COLOR MAGIC
MAGIC
for Beginners

About the Author

Richard Webster is the author of over 75 books and one of New Zealand's most prolific authors. His bestselling books include *Spirit Guides & Angel Guardians* and the new *Creative Visualization for Beginners*, and he is the author of *Soul Mates, Is Your Pet Psychic?, Practical Guide to Past-Life Memories, Astral Travel for Beginners, Miracles*, and the four-book series on archangels *Michael, Gabriel, Raphael*, and *Uriel*.

A noted psychic, Richard is a member of the National Guild of Hypnotherapists (USA), Association of Professional Hypnotherapists and Parapsychologists (UK), International Registry of Professional Hypnotherapists (Canada), and the Psychotherapy and Hypnotherapy Institute of New Zealand. When not touring, he resides in New Zealand with his wife and family.

COLOR
MAGIC
for Beginners

Simple Techniques to Brighten &
Empower Your Life

Richard Webster

Llewellyn Publications
Woodbury, Minnesota

Cover images © Comstock Images
Cover design by Lisa Novak
Edited by Connie Hill
Llewellyn is a registered trademark of Llewellyn Worldwide, Ltd.

ISBN-13: 978-0-7387-0886-7

Llewellyn Publications
A Division of Llewellyn Worldwide, Ltd.
2143 Wooddale Drive, Dept. 0-7387-0886-0
Woodbury, Minnesota 55125-2989, U.S.A.

Printed in the United States of America

Other Books by Richard Webster

For my granddaughter,
Ava Georgia Martin

Contents

Contents

INTRODUCTION

Some years ago, a friend invited me to see his new business premises. He had employed a color consultant to redecorate the building, and was hoping that it would improve productivity. It was fascinating to walk from room to room and feel the effects that different colors create.

Everyone is subliminally aware of the effects of certain colors. We all know that red, for instance, is stimulating and exciting. It is frequently used in fast food restaurants, as it encourages people to eat quickly and then leave, providing room for new customers. I was shy as a child and avoided the color red, as I instinctively knew it attracted attention. That was years before I learned that extroverts generally prefer the warmer colors, while introverts prefer the cooler shades.

The first time I appeared on television I was pleased to spend time in the green room beforehand. This is because green is a calming color that helps people to relax before appearing on the program.

One of my classrooms at high school was painted bright yellow, and I sometimes had headaches while attending lessons there. Yellow is a mentally stimulating color, but too much yellow can cause agitation and headaches.

I was interested in what my friend was trying to do, but found it sad that his only interest in color was in trying to increase productivity. Although he was not aware of it, he had done one positive thing for his employees. The factory walls had originally been painted blue, and his workers frequently complained about feeling cold. The walls were painted orange in the new color scheme, and everyone immediately felt warmer. Of course, this also benefited my friend, as it meant that everyone worked harder, as well.

We live in a world that is vibrant with color, yet most of the time we scarcely notice it. Here's an experiment. Look around the room you are in. See, really see, the color of the walls, furniture, carpet, and the clothes you are wearing. Each of these has an effect upon you, whether you are aware of it or not. You can change your mood and enhance your life by surrounding yourself with colors that are good for you.

Colors have three main aspects. They possess healing qualities. Consequently, color healing has been practiced for thousands of years. Colors also have a psychological effect on us that influences our minds and emotions. There is also an esoteric side to color. This can be utilized in color magic and to help encourage spiritual growth and development.

Most of the time, we are not really aware of the colors around us. After enjoying a pleasant walk, we probably return home feeling refreshed and invigorated, but are unlikely to think about the effects the different colors we saw created in us. It might be different if we choose to walk in a beautiful garden, but even then, we probably enjoy the different colors we see, but again take no notice of the effects they create in us. Every color has an effect on us. Red provides energy and enthusiasm. Green provides healing. Yellow enhances the intellect. Orange provides balance. Blue aids communication, and violet helps us make contact with our souls.

Everyone has color preferences, and children often ask their friends what their favorite colors are. Different systems of character analysis have been devised that use the subject's color preferences. Color clearly reveals our personalities, hopes and dreams.

Color has been used for healing purposes for at least 4,000 years. The ancient Egyptians had color-healing temples at Luxor and Heliopolis. Some people speculate that color healing is even older than that, and that priests in Atlantis were the first to use color-healing techniques.

Knowledge that light was essential to existence must have come extremely early in the history of mankind. Ancient hieroglyphics, jewelry and amulets clearly show the interest these people had in color. Color also had other associations. Around the world, people of different races gave colors to each of the cardinal directions.

In China, for instance, black was the color given to the north, while the south received red. East was green, and west was white. The Tibetans had the four-sided Sumur Mountain, which was home to their gods. The northern slopes of this mountain were given yellow, the southern blue, east white, and west red.

The people of ancient Greece and Rome believed that the world consisted of four elements: Fire, Earth, Air, and Water. Red symbolized Fire, blue symbolized Earth, yellow symbolized Air, and green symbolized Water. Josephus (c. 37–100 C.E.), the Jewish historian, writer, and soldier, associated red with Fire, white with Earth, yellow with Air, and purple with Water. Nearly fifteen hundred years later, Leonardo da Vinci (1452–1519) associated red with Fire, yellow with Earth, blue with Air, and green with Water.

In the late nineteenth century, American ethnologist Alice Fletcher published a list of color meanings that she had learned from the Native Americans she was studying. Red symbolized the sun, stone, animal, and vegetable life, and the procreative force. White symbolized consecration.

Blue symbolized wind, moon, water, thunder, lightning, and the West. Yellow symbolized sunlight.[1]

The hidden meanings of color are revealed in phrases such as "green with envy" and "red with rage." Why not blue or yellow? Later, when we discuss the aura, you will see how these sayings originated. These moods can actually be seen in the person's aura.

Physicists describe color as a function of light. Rainbows are created when light is reflected on raindrops, creating a prism. In 1666, a twenty-three-year-old Cambridge University student named Isaac Newton (1642–1727) made an amazing discovery with two prisms he had bought at a fair. He discovered that all color is contained in white light when he observed what occurred when light was refracted through a prism. He allowed a ray of daylight to enter a darkened room through a small hole in the window shade. He placed a prism where the ray would pass through it. This bent, or refracted, the ray of light, breaking it down to its constituent colors, which were clearly displayed on a white wall on the other side of the room. Sir Isaac Newton was able to clearly recognize the colors of red, orange, yellow, green, blue, indigo, and violet. Nowadays it is thought that each of these colors corresponds to part of the range of wavelengths of energy that can be distinguished by the human eye. This is called the visible spectrum. Red has the longest wavelength and violet the shortest. There are other wavelengths of energy on either side of the visible spectrum that we cannot see. We can't see infrared or ultraviolet, for instance.

Light is an electromagnetic vibration because it travels in waves, in the same way that heat and sound does. When we look at something, what we actually see is light being reflected from it. Our eyes recognize hundreds of different shadings of color by distinguishing between the various bands of wavelengths that each color reflects. The color of an object is determined by the wavelengths it reflects. The other wavelengths are absorbed by the object.

Isaac Newton already knew that passing light through a prism created a rainbow of colors. However, he was the first person to take the experiment to the next stage. He placed a second prism upside down in the path of the rainbow of colors. The colors emerged from this second prism as a single ray of white light. Not everyone appreciated Sir Isaac Newton's genius. John Keats (1795–1821), the famous English poet, wrote that Newton had "destroyed all the poetry of the rainbow by reducing it to prismatic colours."

Until I learned that he was an alchemist, I'd thought it remarkable that Sir Isaac Newton had discovered seven colors in the rainbow. Sir Isaac Newton increased the number of colors in the rainbow from five to seven by adding orange and indigo. His choice of seven colors is probably related to the fact that there were seven known planets, seven days of the week, seven musical notes, and even seven deadly sins. Not surprisingly, Sir Isaac Newton wanted the rainbow to contain a similar number. Newton could have increased the number of colors even more by adding the turquoise that appears between green and blue, or differentiated between light and dark violet, but that would have lost the mystical "seven."

Colors may be differing wavelengths of light, but that would mean nothing if our eyes could not distinguish between them. Light enters the eye through the pupil, which expands or contracts to admit more or less light into the eye. This light is then focused on the retina, at the back of the eye. The retina is composed of millions of specialized cells, including a layer of rods and cones called photoreceptors. There are about one hundred million rods and six and a half million cones in each eye. The rods enable us to distinguish shapes and forms in faint light, but only in black and white. The cones need more light to work with and allow us to see colors. This is why we find it hard to determine color at night.

The photoreceptors in each eye send their findings to the brain, which somehow converts them back into a single image. There is a great deal about this process that scientists have yet to learn. They know that the rods contain disks of a pigment called rhodopsin that is sensitive to light. However, they can only theorize as to how the cones work. They know that the cones contain a light-sensitive pigment called iodopsin, but have not yet been able to explain its function.

The brain plays a vital role in our ability to see color. Stroke victims who have suffered partial brain damage, but have perfectly good eyesight, sometimes see in black and white. The brain also ensures that colors remain consistent and are correctly identified in varying lighting conditions.[2] People who are colorblind can see colors, but confuse colors that most people find easy to distinguish. The vast majority of people who are color blind confuse red with green, but see blue correctly.

It appears that we all see color slightly differently, but despite this, we all feel the effects that different colors have on us. E. Schachtel, a New York psychoanalyst, wrote: "Colors are not only and usually not even primarily 'recognized' but they are *felt* as exciting or soothing, dissonant or harmonious . . . joyous or somber, warm or cool, disturbing and distracting or conducive to concentration and tranquility."[3]

We all experience the effects that color has on us, but some people sense this in different ways. Some people perceive different colors in pain, or the letters of the alphabet. Many years ago, I lived with someone who perceived colors when listening to music. This is known as synaesthesia, or color hearing. Until I got used to it, it was disconcerting to hear a piece of music being described as "light blue" or "campfire smoke gray." Most of the time, he experienced cheerful pieces as light colors, while more somber music was experienced as darker shades. My friend is not alone in this.

Russian composer Alexander Scriabin (1872–1915) was a synaesthetic and associated musical keys with color. He saw the key of C as red, and G as orange. *Prometheus*, a work he wrote for a "color organ," was performed in 1910. To the surprise of his audience, the work was performed with an accompaniment of colored lights.

Jean Sibelius (1865–1957), the Finnish composer, was also synaesthetic. When someone asked him what color he would like his stove to be repainted in, he replied, "F Major." Fortunately, the stove was painted green, which was the color Sibelius wanted.[4]

Russian artist Wassily Kandinsky (1866–1944) said: "The sound of colors is so definite that it would be hard to find anyone who would try to express bright yellow in the bass notes, or [a] dark lake in the treble."[5]

French composer Olivier Messiaen (1908–1992) explained how he saw and heard color: "I am all the same affected by a kind of synopsia, found more in my mind than in my body, which allows me, when I hear music, and equally when I read it, to see inwardly in the mind's eye, colors in an extremely vivid manner."[6]

Children are extremely good at experiencing different colors as sounds, shapes, tastes, and emotions. Here is a short poem that my granddaughter Eden wrote when she was seven years old:

Shy is light pink,
It tastes like soft butter,
It sounds like people writing slowly,
It feels like cotton,
It smells like a freshly bought quilt.

Some people can feel colors with their hands. Many blind people have developed this ability, but I have also come across a number of sighted people who are able to do this. A small number of people associate colors with scents and tastes. Although there is currently no conclusive evidence of how synaesthesia works, it appears that the centers that process sensory information in the brain are linked, and it is this that allows some people to see colors and relate them to sound, touch, scent, or taste.

Some people also associate different colors to letters of the alphabet, and even days of the week. Tricia Guild, a well-known British color consultant, has always associated colors to different days of the week. In her book, *Tricia Guild on Colour*, she wrote that she has "since early childhood, experienced days of the week as particular colours: Monday is pale blue; Thursday is lime green; Friday is brown; Sunday is pink."[7]

Over the years, a large number of color tests have been devised to determine people's personalities according to their color preferences. The best known of these is the Lüscher Color Test, devised by Max Lüscher, a Swiss psychologist, in 1947. The full test involves forty-three color samples, though it is more usually performed with just eight. Max Lüscher believed that the four basic colors of red, blue, green and yellow depicted different biological states, and that a healthy person would place all four of these in the first five positions. The grouping of different colors was also analyzed to determine the results.

Once you understand the power behind different colors, you will be able to harness them to achieve your goals. That is "color magic," the topic of this book.

CHAPTER ONE

A RAINBOW OF COLOR

Every day you make color choices. You may decide to wear a particular outfit because you have an important meeting to go to. This choice may be made consciously or unconsciously. If you need confidence for any reason, you might deliberately choose red. However, if you knew you were going to be dealing with difficult people, you might unconsciously decide to wear blue. Instinctively, you would be making the right color choice.

You even make color choices with your food. You might choose a red apple in preference to a yellow banana. This may have nothing to do with taste, but be a subconscious decision based on the right color for you at that time. Incidentally, you should eat foods of many different colors to keep your body healthy.

After breakfast, you'll brush your teeth. What color is your toothbrush? What made you choose a toothbrush of that particular color?

You might drive to work in your own car. Why did you choose a car of that particular color? As you go to work you might see green grass and a blue sky. You'll certainly see many different colored vehicles on the road.

You may not have a great deal of choice in the color scheme at your place of work, but the chances are that you can add different colors by personalizing your workspace with potted plants, ornaments and photographs.

All day long you're being exposed to a variety of different colors. These colors affect every aspect of your being. The psychological effects that colors have on people have been studied for many years. The colors of fire, such as red, orange and yellow, make us feel warm. This is not just a psychological effect, as scientists have demonstrated that under a red light we secrete more adrenaline, our blood pressure and rate of breathing increase, and our temperature rises slightly. The opposite occurs under blue lighting. We consider blue and green to be cooling colors.

Even young children are aware of the psychological effects that different colors produce. They usually relate red to anger, aggression, and excitement, while green is related to peace and quietness. In 1978 a study was undertaken in which children were asked to color in a shape while looking at happy and sad pictures. They used orange, yellow, green and blue while looking at the happy pictures, but chose brown, black and red while looking at the sad ones.[1]

People also have personal color preferences, and these vary as we go through life. All around the world young children like red best. Only after the age of eight do children express a preference for cool colors. Not surprisingly, extroverted adolescents like red, while their quieter, more reserved compatriots prefer blue. More than half of all adults in the Western world say that blue is their favorite color.[2] Only in Spain is red placed before blue and yellow as a favorite color. Elderly people prefer light colors, but find yellow the least appealing.

There may be a geographical basis on which colors people like best. In an experiment, Scandinavian people indicated a preference for blue and green, while people from Mediterranean countries preferred the warmer colors.[3]

Let's start by looking at the basic meanings of the colors you see most frequently.

Red

As red is the color of blood, it is considered to be the color of life. It is stimulating, vital, enthusiastic, energetic and passionate. If you are "red-blooded," you possess these qualities. It is intense and has a strong desire to achieve. Shakespeare wrote: "My love is like a red, red rose," as it is also the color of love. This is why red flowers are so popular on Valentine's Day. Red is a powerful color that is related to conquest and success. This is why we "roll out the red car-pet" for important dignitaries. Important things happen on "red-letter days." If you won the lottery and bought your-self a sports car, you would probably request that it be red. This is because a red sports car symbolizes all the qualities we have mentioned.

When red is used positively it is fun loving, creative, am-bitious, persistent, and motivated. It symbolizes strength, power, and self-confidence.

Interesting Facts About Red

The word red is derived from two words: the Sanskrit *rud-hira* and the Anglo-Saxon *read*.

Red is associated with the planet Mars, which was named after the Roman god of war (who drove a red chariot). Red was also the color of the Russian Revolution, which is why the communists were called "Reds."

When red is used negatively it is destructive. An angry person "sees red." When someone is caught "red-handed," they are committing a crime. The very term "red-handed" conjures up an image of blood on the hands. In the seven-teenth century, adulteresses in New England had to wear a scarlet letter A to compound their shame and disgrace. In the Bible we read: "Though your sins be as scarlet, they shall be as white as snow; though they be red like crimson, they shall be as wool." (Isaiah 1:18) As red attracts immedi-ate attention, it is used on stoplights and on signs indicat-ing danger. At one time, red-haired and red-bearded people were viewed with suspicion. This is because Judas Iscariot was believed to have red hair.

Red is useful for people who want to lose weight, as it stimulates the pituitary gland and speeds up the assimilation of food.

Insurance company records show that red-colored cars are more likely to be involved in accidents than cars of other colors. However, there is also a tradition that says that a red ribbon should be tied inside all new cars to promote luck and safe driving.

Cardinals wear red vestments to remind them of the blood spilled by the Christian martyrs. The ancient Greeks wore red robes when acting the *Iliad* to remind them of the blood spilled in battle.

The legendary philosopher's stone, which was sought after by medieval alchemists because they believed it cured disease and transformed base metals into gold, was thought to be red in color.

The Hebrew people consider red the color of sacrifice and sin. Red symbolizes the blood of Christ for Christians. Consequently, it was sometimes worn by martyrs.

Orange

Orange is exciting, assertive, joyful, and persistent. It balances the life-force color of red with the lightness and goal-setting qualities of yellow. This combines physical energy with the power of thought, providing the potential for wisdom as well as achievement. Orange encourages new ideas and new ways of looking at things. It is thoughtful and considerate, as well as energetic. Orange symbolizes warmth, expansion, prosperity, harvest, tolerance, and love for all life.

Orange is usually positive. However, when it is used negatively, it can be sensual, self-indulgent, lazy, and lacking in energy.

Orange is virile and is useful for people who need more force and drive.

Interesting Facts About Orange

Oranges were not imported into Europe until medieval times. Until the seventeenth century, the word orange was associated only with the fruit. Items that were orange in color were called red, yellow, or gold. At about the same time, orange gained an erotic connotation. This is because the people of the day believed that Nell Gwynne (c.1650–1687) seduced King Charles II (1630–1685) with the oranges she sold.

In ancient Rome, people used bleach and henna to create red and orange hair, which was considered highly fashionable.

Orange was the color of the early Christian church, as oranges symbolized the fruits of the earth.

In Northern Ireland, the Protestants who want to remain part of the United Kingdom are called the Orangemen, after the orange-colored flowers they have worn in their parades since 1795.

Yellow

Yellow is lighthearted, carefree, and full of the joys of life. It is warm, bright, and cheerful. It is also intellectual, provides hope, and helps people find a sense of direction in their lives. The only disadvantage of this approach is that yellow relies much more on logic and thought than it does on feelings and emotions. However, yellow is always learning and striving for knowledge and wisdom.

Interesting Facts About Yellow

Yellow is sometimes considered a negative color. The actor playing the role of the devil in medieval morality plays always wore yellow. Cowards are called "yellow." When this color is used negatively it can lead to cowardice, jealousy, treason, treachery, dishonor, and perversion. These associations came about because medieval artists believed that Judas Iscariot wore yellow robes. In Nazi Germany, Jewish people were made to wear yellow armbands. Victims of the Inquisition were also made to wear yellow armbands.

However, in China yellow was the imperial color and was considered highly auspicious. Lucky charms were often printed on yellow paper.

Green

Green is soothing, restful, and nurturing. It provides balance and restores body, mind, and soul. It is the color of nature, and symbolizes growth and abundance. It is also the color of renewal, which relates it to hope and longevity. It is also related to calmness, stability, peace, empathy, and contentment. It has always been associated with healing. It is hard working, conscientious, reliable, and sometimes stubborn.

Interesting Facts About Green

The word green comes from the Anglo-Saxon *grene*, which derives in turn from the old German *gro* for growth.

Green is associated with growth, which is why a "green-horn," or someone who is "green" or "green around the gills," is inexperienced, as they are not yet fully grown. Tom Brown, the hero of the nineteenth-century novels *Tom Brown's Schooldays* and *Tom Brown at Oxford* by Thomas Hughes, was described as "very green for being puzzled at so simple a matter."

Many actors are superstitious about green. Despite this, they are happy to wait in the "green room" before going on-stage. This superstition began when stages were lit by lime-lights. The lights burned lime, which produced a greenish light that made anything green almost invisible. Actors also do not like wearing green onstage. Two reasons have been suggested to account for this. The first is that stage lights make green clothing look unflattering. The other reason is that fairies and leprechauns like green, and they might cause mischief to anyone who dares to wear it.

It is not only people in the acting profession who dis-like green. Mario Andretti, the famous racing car driver, would not allow green to be used in any of his clothes or equipment.[4]

Sailors also have a fear of green and consider it highly unlucky. Even Winston Churchill was affected by this superstition. It is said that when he visited the fishing community of Hull, England, during World War II, he paid a man ten pounds to dispose of a green sweater.[5] A possible explanation for this superstition is that green is the color of nature. However, everything ultimately dies, and so green turns to black. Consequently, to avoid turning black (dying), all you need do is avoid wearing green.

Green is considered a lucky color in Ireland, and leprechauns wear green. A children's sing-along game in Ireland discusses what to wear at a funeral. After the words: "Shall we come in green?" the response is: "Green is for the good people. You cannot come in that." The good people are, of course, leprechauns.

As plants are green, green is also believed to symbolize the resurrection.

Blue

Blue is the coolest color, and has a calming effect. It is associated with truth, sincerity, loyalty, justice, and intelligence. Traditionally, Mary, the mother of Jesus, wore a blue cloak to symbolize her love, loyalty, and devotion. (In medieval times, artists considered red to be the color of God, blue the color of the Son of God, and consequently of Mary as well, and green for the Holy Spirit.) Today, businesspeople frequently wear blue as it denotes confidence and stability.

Interesting Facts About Blue

The word blue is derived from both the French *bleu* and the German *blau*.

Blue has some strange connotations. A "blue story" is one that's licentious. "Bluebeard" is a synonym for a murderous husband. Blue has also been associated with melancholy ("feeling blue" and "blue Monday"), and this might be where blues music received its name. "Blue-collar" workers are laborers, but "bluestockings" are intellectuals. We sometimes experience good luck "out of the blue." Someone who is loyal or faithful is termed "true-blue."

It would be hard to find a bride who didn't walk down the aisle without "something old, something new, something borrowed, and something blue." The old item should have caused "luck" to someone in the past, the new object brings hope to the bride, the borrowed object carries the lender's blessing and good luck, and the blue object banishes all evil spirits from the wedding day and the entire marriage.

Philosophers in ancient Rome wore blue in their robes to indicate spirituality and wisdom. Druid bards also wore blue to symbolize harmony and truth. Blue still denotes philosophy in the American university system today.

Wearing blue traditionally protected people from witches, as it was believed that blue was the color of heaven, and witches didn't like it. It also protected the person from the effect of the evil eye.

Another traditional belief about blue relates it to luck. Children have a rhyme that goes:

Touch blue
And your wish
Will come true.

The Order of the Garter, which is the highest form of knighthood in Great Britain, was established after King Edward III stooped to pick up a blue garter that had been dropped by one of the ladies at court.

The term "blue blood" is given to people of high birth, and originally comes from Spain. The aristocrats with no Moorish ancestors possessed veins that looked bluer than those who had a mixed ancestry.

Mosquitoes are attracted to blue more than any other color.

Indigo

Indigo is associated with calmness, dignity, idealism, justice, wisdom, and service to humanity. It is also related to inspiration, intuition, and spirituality.

Interesting Facts About Indigo

The word indigo is derived from a Greek term that means "from India."

Indigo was originally obtained from the woad plant and was a popular color in ancient Greece, Egypt, and India. It was also known in ancient Asia and Peru.

The British Museum in London has a tablet of Babylonian dye recipes, showing how popular the color indigo was 2,700 years ago.

Before 1900, indigo was obtained solely from the *Indigofera* and *Isatis* genera of plants. Until the beginning of the twentieth century, India exported large quantities of indigo dye extracted from these plants. The chemical structure of indigo was discovered in 1883 by Adolf von Baeyer, and a commercially feasible method of manufacturing a synthetic form of indigo was invented in the late 1890s.

Violet

Violet is associated with inspiration, spirituality, and the sacred. Violet is selfless, loving, tolerant, and intuitive. It enhances the imagination.

Interesting Facts About Violet

The word violet comes from the Old French *violete*, which is a plant that produces a flower of this color. Purple comes from the Latin *purpura*. This was a mollusk that the Tyrian purple dye came from. Purple was an imperial color in ancient Rome.

Violet and purple are generally considered to be the same color, although some people believe that violet is slightly redder than purple.

The Greek priests at Eleusis wore purple or violet robes. This shows how long spiritual qualities have been associated with violet. In Christianity, violet symbolizes the Passion of Christ, and is the color of Advent and Holy Week.

Some people believe that Jesus wore purple garments when he was crucified.[6]

Violet flowers were used in ancient festivals because people believed that they would protect them from headaches and drunkenness.

At one time, newborn babies were wrapped in purple cloth to encourage future fame, wealth, and success.[7]

It is interesting to note that the U.S. military decoration, the Purple Heart, is awarded to soldiers who are wounded or killed in action. This decoration was established by George Washington in 1782, and was originally presented to recognize exceptional military merit. The choice of purple as the color is most likely because it exemplifies the extraordinary nature of the effort that warranted it.

The term "purple prose" is used to describe florid, ornate, or hyperbolic language. The color purple is rich and vivid, and this has become related to the exaggerated style of writing that bears its name. People are also described as being "purple with rage" when they are extremely angry.

Pink

Pink is nurturing and loving. It is gentle, compassionate, self-sacrificing, and giving. It relates to femininity and innocence. It is a positive and cheerful color, which is why we describe a happy person as being "in the pink."

Interesting Facts About Pink

In English country lore, pink is believed to encourage happy thoughts about the future. The phrase "tickled pink" probably relates to this. People who are "in the pink" are believed to be happy and healthy. However, if someone is described as being a "pinko," it is because they are thought to have extremely left-wing views.

Pink has a calming effect, and in the United States there are at least 1,500 hospitals and correctional institutions with a pink room that is used to calm down violent and emotionally disturbed people.[8]

White

White is the color of purity, innocence, and protection. It provides sensations of freedom and unlimited opportunities. White eliminates negativity, and encourages forgiveness and acceptance. This is where the term "the white dove of peace" came from.

Interesting Facts About White

"White magic" is magic that is performed with a positive goal in mind. It harms no one, but helps all. A "white lie" is an untruth that is either harmless, or is said to avoid hurting someone's feelings.

Priests frequently wear white robes, as the color signifies spirit and light. Freshly baptized Christians also wear white clothes to signify their purity after being born again. This association also carries through to the tradition of brides being married in white. At the Transfiguration, Christ's robes were "exceeding white as snow" (Mark 9:3). White also signifies forgiveness. In Isaiah 1:18, the Lord says: "Though your sins be as scarlet, they shall be as white as snow."

A "white elephant" is an object that costs much more than it's worth and is difficult to dispose of. This term is credited to one of the kings of Siam, who gave a white elephant to any courtier he wished to ruin financially.

In the seventeenth century the Bourbons used a white flag to symbolize a legitimate cause. However, the meaning of a white flag gradually changed and it became a sign of surrender. This comes from the white feather that symbolizes a coward or poor fighter.

A "whited sepulchre" is a hypocrite. (Matthew 23:27) To "whitewash" something is to cover it up to make everything appear above board.

The most famous white building in the world is the White House in Washington, D.C. In 1800, the decision was made that the building had to be white, the same color as the ancient Greek buildings. Half a century later, scholars found that the ancient Greek buildings were not white at all, but had been painted in a large variety of colors.

Brown

The word brown comes from the Anglo-Saxon *brun*.

Brown, the color of earth and of fall, is a grounding color. It symbolizes good health, hard work, stability, and reward through effort. Brown enhances all of the other colors.

In the Middle Ages, brown was a color customarily used in mourning.

Interesting Facts About Brown

Christian monks often wear brown garments, as they associate it with poverty, humility, and renunciation. This symbolism is derived from humble clay. In China, the emperors of the Sung dynasty had a completely different view of the color. The color brown was used to symbolize the dynasty.

Brown was an extremely popular color for men and women's clothing during the Great Depression. This was because it naturally concealed any dirty marks. Sigmund Freud, not the most cheerful of people at the best of times, thought that the main symbolism for brown was excrement.

Black

Black is sophisticated, powerful, and mysterious. Although we call it a color, black is created by the absence of light, and therefore color. Black absorbs light but reflects none back.

Interesting Facts About Black

Black traditionally has negative connotations. This is why we have terms such as blackball, blacklist, blackmail, black magic, and black market. Despite this, if you're "in the black," you're making a profit.

A "black sheep" is someone who causes embarrassment because he doesn't fit in with the rest of the group he belongs to. "Black magic" is magic performed for an evil purpose. Priests wear black as a sign of respectability. However, the tradition of wearing black at a funeral was not originally done as a sign of respect for the deceased. It is a continuation of an old Roman custom that says that, in the presence of death, we are totally insignificant.[9] However, it may also have been intended to make the survivors invisible to the spirit who had taken away the soul of the deceased.

A black cat can indicate either good or bad luck, depending on your beliefs. At one time, people believed that witches could transform themselves into cats. Naturally, these cats would be black, as this color was believed to be evil. Consequently, if a black cat walked across their path, these people would think that it could easily be a witch. In the thirteenth century, Pope Gregory IX associated black cats with witchcraft. People believed it could be the devil in disguise. When the Order of the Knights Templar was suppressed in the early fourteenth century, its members, after being tortured, were forced to confess that they worshipped the devil in the form of a black cat. Fortunately, black cats have not fared as badly in other parts of the world. The Japanese consider black cats to be a sign of good luck, and Buddhists believe that a dark-haired cat in the house indicates future prosperity. Today, although some people still believe that a black cat walking in front of them is a sign of bad luck, many also believe that a black cat walking toward them is a sign of good fortune. Needless to say, cat lovers love all cats, no matter what color they happen to be.

Silver

Silver balances and harmonizes. It is related to the moon and symbolizes change, learning, and femininity. It can be detached and somewhat introspective.

Interesting Facts About Silver

Because silver has always been associated with the moon, it became associated with hope, wisdom, and eloquence. This is why a good speaker is described as being "silver-tongued." The Chinese have a saying that relates to this: "Speech is silver, silence golden." If you're born "with a silver spoon in your mouth," you're distinguished from the time you were born. A cloud with a "silver lining" is a sign that the future will be much brighter than the present.

At times, silver has had a negative connotation. This is because Jesus Christ was betrayed for "thirty pieces of silver."

Gold

Gold relates to success, abundance, and power, tempered by wisdom. It is positive, self-motivated, and generous.

Interesting Facts About Gold

Gold has always been valuable and valued. In ancient times, it was believed that gods were the color of gold. It was also believed to be a residue of the sun. Gold is considered a masculine symbol because of its association with the sun.

Now that you've looked at the main colors it is time to examine some techniques that will enable you to harness the powerful energies the colors provide. We'll start looking at that in the next chapter.

CHAPTER TWO

THE POWER OF COLOR

Color therapy works on the basis that colors have a beneficial effect on the workings of different organs in the body.
If a particular organ is afflicted in some way, a color therapist will expose the person's body to the specific color that
has the most beneficial effect on the organ.

Interestingly, we often do this subconsciously, by wearing clothes or eating foods of a certain color. If someone is
recovering from a broken relationship, for instance, he or
she might start wearing more green. Although the person
may not realize that green will help him or her to get over
the broken relationship and start moving ahead again, he
or she will simply feel a need to wear green.

You can also do this consciously. If you need more energy, you should wear some red. If you wish to enhance your connection with the divine, violet will prove helpful. It is more effective if the color is visible, but if the color you need does not fit in or seem appropriate to what you are doing, you can wear it as an undergarment, or carry it as a swatch of cloth or a handkerchief.

Your Color Collection

It is a good idea to collect samples of each of the colors of the rainbow. You might create these yourself, using cardboard and colored pens. Alternatively, you might cut squares of the different colors from magazines, or use the color charts put out by paint or printing ink manufacturers. A friend of mine has a collection of colored tiles that she uses.

Sit down quietly, somewhere where you are unlikely to be disturbed for at least thirty minutes. Look at each of the colors in turn, and see which one you are drawn to. It might take a few minutes to discover which is the right color for you at that moment. This is not a conscious choice. It is more a feeling that a certain color is what you need.

Place the other colors out of sight, and gaze at the color you instinctively chose. Take several slow, deep breaths, and let your mind and body relax. There is no need to think about anything in particular. Simply focus on the color and allow your body, mind, and spirit to absorb that color's energy.

Your body will tell you when you've absorbed enough. Once you start to feel restless, or lose interest, stop. You will notice a profound difference when you get up after this experiment. Although you were not consciously aware that your body was craving a certain color, you will notice the results immediately. If you were angry, you will have calmed down. If you were lethargic and unmotivated, you will suddenly have all the energy you need to perform a certain task. If you were feeling sad or lonely, you'll feel more cheerful and positive.

My friend who has the collection of colored tiles does this experiment in a different way. Every morning she looks at her collection of tiles and chooses the tile that seems appropriate for her for that day. She props this tile up on her desk, so that she is exposed to its energies throughout the day. At times, she will look at the tile, but most of the time she will be hard at work, and will absorb the energies of the color subliminally. Sometimes she might use the same tile for three or four days in a row, but usually the color changes from day to day.

The Power of Imagination

If you want to experiment with color at a time when you do not have your color samples with you, all you need do is close your eyes and imagine them. Go through all the colors, one by one, and ask yourself about each one. "Do I need more red at this time?" "How about orange? Yellow?" And so on. Once you have chosen a specific color, imagine yourself breathing in pure red (or whatever the color happens to be). Continue doing this until you feel that you have absorbed enough of that color's energy. You will find that this works just as well as the former exercise. However, it is better to familiarize yourself with the method using the color samples first, before experimenting with the exercise without.

Candle Burning

In my book *Candle Magic for Beginners,* I mentioned a friend who burns candles every Sunday evening while writing in her journal. She knows nothing about color, but instinctively burns candles that provide her with the color or colors she needs at that time.

You can do what my friend does, and choose the right candle colors intuitively. You can also deliberately burn a candle or candles of a color that you happen to need. If you were concerned about a particular situation that you need to handle, for instance, you should burn red candles, as this will give you the confidence that you need.

You should choose your candles carefully when entertaining a group of people. Your guests will be quieter and more introspective if you have violet candles on your table. Yellow candles will make them more outgoing and conversational.

Kombolois

Kombolois are used as worry beads in Greece. The name is derived from the Greek word *kombos,* which means a knot, and *loi,* which means a group. They are believed to have been introduced to Greece during the Turkish occupation, and were first used by the monks in the monasteries on Mount Athos.

A komboloi is a strand of beads tied in a circle. The number of beads is unimportant, but the usual number is between 16 and 23. Unlike rosary beads, komboloi beads are loose on the strand, which means that they can click together. This clicking sound is part of the attraction that kombolois hold. A tassel is frequently attached to the knot that joins the two ends. Kombolois are made from a variety of materials, and antique ones, made from expensive gemstones, sell for large sums of money.

Kombolois are readily available from stores that import products from Greece, and are also available over the Internet. However, it is not hard to make your own.

All you need is a selection of beads that fit loosely onto a length of cord. The beads can be any size you wish. I like larger, heavier beads, but that is simply a personal preference. I have several kombolois, one each of the seven colors of the rainbow. I also have a multi-colored komboloi, which I use when I feel I need the energy from a number of colors.

To make your komboloi, start by tying a knot at one end of the length of cord. This has to be larger than the hole in the beads, to prevent them falling off the end. Thread the first bead onto the cord and allow it to drop down to the knot. Thread the cord through the hole in the bead one more time to create a fixed bead. This is the only bead that is treated this way. Thread the other beads onto the cord. Once you have done this, tie the two ends of the cord together, creating a circle. Tie a tassel or lucky charm to the knotted area.

Your komboloi is now ready to use. The traditional method is to hang the komboloi from the middle finger of your non-dominant hand, with your palm upward. The knot, fixed bead and tassel of the komboloi should be resting on your fingers, with the other beads suspended below your hand. Gently swing and flip the beads, so they come around your first finger and land on the palm of your hand. With your thumb, push one bead at a time off your palm. As each bead drops to join the others it will hit the next bead in line, creating a hypnotic clicking sound. Once all the beads have been pushed off your hand, flip the komboloi again, and repeat the process. The process sounds harder than it is. With just a little bit of practice, you will be able to do this automatically, without looking at your hand. Playing with your komboloi in this way is extremely restful, and you will quickly enter into a relaxed, meditative state. It is easy to see why they are used as worry beads, as they soothe the mind and eliminate feelings of stress and tension.

Some people prefer to hold their komboloi between their hands and gently hit the beads together to create the clicking sound. I prefer the traditional method, as I enjoy the rhythmical sound and the gentle movement of the hand. However, you should feel free to use them in any way that seems right for you.

If I feel the need for a specific color, I pick up my komboloi of the same color and play with it for several minutes. At the end of this time I feel relaxed, rested, revitalized and full of the energy of the color I needed. Kombolois can also be used to encourage clairvoyance and precognition, as the process of playing with the beads allows you to enter into a relaxed, mystical state that enables psychic perceptions to occur.

Dowsing for Color

You can also dowse for the color that your body needs. Dowsing is most often used to locate underground water, but it has many other uses. You will need a pendulum for this experiment. You can buy attractive pendulums at any New Age or crystal store. A small piece of clear quartz attached to a length of cord or chain would be ideal. However, any small weight attached to several inches of chain, thread, or cord will work.

Hold the cord between the forefinger and thumb of your dominant hand (right hand if you're right-handed, left if you're left-handed). Sit down, and rest the elbow of the arm you are using on a table, allowing the weight to hang freely an inch or so above the surface of the table.

Stop the movements of the pendulum with your free hand, and then ask the pendulum which direction indicates "yes." Remain positively expectant, and wait for the pendulum to move. It will move in one of four directions. It might go in a straight line from side to side, or toward and away from you. Alternatively, it might make a circular movement, either clockwise or counterclockwise.

Once you have determined which direction indicates "yes," stop the pendulum's movement, and then ask which direction indicates "no." You still have two possible directions left. Ask which movement denotes "I don't know," and "I don't want to answer."

Once you have determined the meanings for each direction, you should test the pendulum by asking it questions that you know the answers to. You might, for instance, ask if you are male. The pendulum will give a positive response if you are, and a negative response if you aren't. You will find the pendulum a useful tool that will answer any questions that can be answered by one of the four movements.

It might take several minutes to determine all of this the first time you do it. With practice, though, you will find the pendulum moving almost instantly, as soon as you ask it a question. If you have any problems with the pendulum, experiment by holding the cord in different positions to make it shorter or longer. You might also experiment by using the pendulum in your other hand. Most people find it much easier to operate a pendulum with their dominant hand, but a few people obtain better results with the other hand. Once the pendulum has moved, you will have no difficulty in getting it to work whenever you wish.

After you have become used to the pendulum, you can use it to determine which color you need. Start by asking it if you need to absorb more red energy. Wait for a response, and then ask about each of the other colors in turn. You may find that you need two or three colors, depending on your state of health, energy levels, and what is going on in your life.

When the pendulum has told you what you need, you can then use the methods described earlier to absorb the color or colors you need.

Color Visualization

When you visualize something, you imagine it in your mind. Some people "see" vivid pictures in their minds. Others see faintly or not at all, but experience the visualization in different ways. In this visualization, you will imagine a color in your mind, and then see what thoughts and feelings come into your mind. You will gain a number of insights into the color you are visualizing, and are likely to be surprised at what occurs to you while performing this exercise.

All you need do is sit down comfortably, close your eyes, and take several slow deep breaths. Allow yourself to relax as much as possible. Once you feel totally relaxed, visualize or imagine a color in your mind. It makes no difference what color you choose. Feel and sense this color as clearly as possible. Imagine that you are completely surrounded by it. Notice if the color feels warm or cold. Do you enjoy being surrounded by this color? Does it feel safe and protective? See how you react to this color. What emotions are created in you by this color? Remain as dispassionate as possible, as if you were an outside observer, curious about your feelings and reactions.

Once you have learned everything you need, allow the color to disappear from your mind. Take three slow deep breaths and open your eyes. If you wish, you can close your eyes again and explore another color. I prefer to think about the thoughts, feelings, and sensations that the color has produced for a few minutes before closing my eyes again. If I think there is any possibility that I might forget what has happened, I will write down everything I can think of before continuing.

Fabric Store Visualization

This is another visualization to explore your feelings about different colors. Choose a time and place where you are not likely to be disturbed. Make yourself as comfortable as possible, then close your eyes and take several slow deep breaths. On each exhalation say to yourself: "Relax, relax, relax."

Once you feel completely relaxed, visualize or imagine that you are walking along a street with beautiful, exclusive stores on each side. It is a pleasant, sunny day and you're feeling happy. You pause and look in a few shop windows. You are attracted by the window display in a fabric store and decide to go inside.

You are amazed at how large the store is. The range of fabrics is immense, and you walk through the store admiring the different colors and patterns on the samples on display. In the far corner there is a large display of a single color. It is the color you need. You walk into the center of this display and look around. You are totally surrounded by this color. There is a comfortable chair beside you, and you sit down and allow yourself to experience everything that comes into your mind and body as a result of surrounding yourself in this color.

Remain sitting in the chair for as long as you wish. When you feel ready, get up and walk around the store for a minute or two before leaving. Once you are outside on the street again, you can allow the visualization to fade away. Take three slow deep breaths, and open your eyes.

Spend a few minutes thinking about what occurred to you during the visualization before carrying on with your day. I sometimes perform this visualization in bed at night, and allow myself to drop off to sleep at the end of it. Sometimes I fall asleep while sitting in the comfortable chair surrounded by the color I need.

Body Movement Exercise

Dancing, and moving your body in other ways, is a wonderful physical way to experience the sensations of different colors. Some people are more naturally in tune with their bodies than others, but this exercise can be done by anyone. At one workshop I gave, a man was in a wheelchair. I did not expect him to participate in this exercise, but he proved to be a superb dancer with his hands and arms.

You will need samples of different colors. In my workshops I used fabric samples, as I wanted the colors to be as large as possible. However, size is not of great importance if you are doing this at home on your own.

It is important that you have privacy for this exercise. You want to feel free and uninhibited. This is not always possible to achieve when there are other people in the room. As you will be moving around the room, you should wear loose-fitting clothes. I like to be barefooted for this exercise.

Attach a sample of the color you wish to explore on a plain wall at about head height. Stand a few paces away from it and gaze at the color for a minute or two. When you feel ready, allow your body to move. You may start dancing around the room. You may stand on one spot, but move your arms, legs and bodies in different ways to symbolize the color. You will find that different colors cause you to move in different ways. Feel free to make any movements that seem right. You are exploring the color at a physical level and any and all movements are perfect for you. This is why it is important to have privacy. You will find some colors motivate you to start moving right away, while with others it might seem to be ages before you make any movement at all.

You may experience a strong emotional response with some colors. Express these emotions in any way that feels right for you. You might laugh, cry, become aroused, mourn, feel euphoric, or find long-forgotten memories coming back to you as you move. Movement is a useful way of bringing insights from the subconscious to the conscious mind.

Stop moving when the time seems right for you. You might want to pause and reflect on what you experienced before carrying on with your day. As this exercise is a stimulating one, it is better to perform it at least two hours before going to bed.

I often feel an urge to draw a mandala (see chapter 9) or to write poetry after a session of color body movement. Consequently, this exercise can be used to bolster creativity. However, the main purpose of color movement is to experience the various colors in a completely different way.

Painful Memory Release

This visualization allows you to eliminate the negative effects of painful memories. It might be an occasion when you felt slighted in some way, someone put you down, or perhaps said something that hurt you. It doesn't matter what the specific memory is. This visualization is designed to help you put it into perspective, and to let it go.

Again, find a quiet place where you will not be interrupted or disturbed. Make yourself as comfortable as possible, take several slow deep breaths, and relax as much as you can. Once you feel totally relaxed, allow yourself to relive the painful memory in your mind. Try to see it as dispassionately as possible, as if it was happening to someone else, rather than you.

Once you have done that, visualize the color red. Once you can clearly see, or imagine, the color in your mind, go through the painful memory again, but this time see it through a red filter. Once you have done this, allow the red color to fade away to nothing. Take three slow deep breaths and then visualize the color orange. Go through your memory again, this time through an orange filter. Repeat the visualization with yellow, green, blue, indigo and violet.

You will notice that the painful memory will appear differently each time. Some colors may make the memory more painful, but others will make the memory appear ridiculous and of no account. Repeat the visualization using only the colors that trivialize the painful memory. Once you have done this, visualize the scene twice more: once through a pink filter, and again with white.

You should repeat this visualization every day until the memory ceases to be hurtful. You will discover which colors increase the pain when you do the visualization for the first time. There is no need to use them again. Use only the colors that diminish the effects of the painful memory, and continue using them until the pain has completely gone.

Every color is important, and we are fortunate to live in a world that is so full of vibrant colors. Naturally, some colors will appeal to you more than others. There are also specific colors that relate to you because of your name and date of birth. These are your personal colors, and we'll look at them in the next chapter.

CHAPTER THREE

YOUR PERSONAL COLORS

Your aura contains all the colors of the rainbow. Consequently, the whole spectrum is present in your body. However, other colors also play an important part in your makeup. These have been known for at least 2,600 years, when Pythagoras came up with his theory that everything in life was based on mathematics. Today, Pythagoras is best known for his theorem, but in his own day he was renowned as a mathematician, philosopher, mystic, and teacher.

In the Pythagorean system of numerology, everyone has three important numbers, derived from their date of birth and their full name at birth. These numbers also relate to colors. Fortunately, these numbers are easy to determine.

Life Path Number

Your Life Path number represents your purpose in this lifetime. It is the sum of your month, day, and year of birth, reduced down to a single digit. There are two exceptions. Whenever you encounter an 11 or 22 you stop reducing the numbers. If you came across 43, for instance, you would add the 4 and the 3 together to create a 7. If you came across an 11, you would not add the 1 and the 1 to make 2.

Here is an example for someone born on July 12, 1973:

7 (month)

12 (day)

1973 (year)

1992, and $1 + 9 + 9 + 2 = 21$, and $2 + 1 = 3$.

This person has a Life Path number of 3.

Here is an example for someone born on February 29, 1944:

2 (month)

29 (day)

1944 (year)

1975, and $1 + 9 + 7 + 5 = 22$

As the 22 does not get reduced to a 4, this person has a Life Path number of 22.

You will notice that I have created a sum out of the person's month, day, and year of birth. This is because the 11 and 22 can sometimes be lost if the numbers are added in a straight line. This is what happens to the person in the previous example:

2 (month) + 2 + 9 (day) + 1 + 9 + 4 + 4 (year) = 31, and 3 + 1 = 4

Once you have determined your Life Path, you can see what color it represents, and also your purpose in life, in the following chart:

1. Red: People on a 1 Life Path need to learn to stand on their own two feet and achieve independence. Once they have done this they have the potential to become pioneers and leaders.

2. Orange: People on a 2 Life Path need to cooperate and harmonize with others. They are caring, loving, intuitive, and highly sensitive.

3. Yellow: People on a 3 Life Path need to express themselves in some sort of way, usually through singing, dancing, writing, or talking. They are positive, enthusiastic people who express all the joys of life.

4. Green: People on a 4 Life Path need to learn the benefits of system and order. They are down-to-earth, capable, hard-working people who work best when they know exactly what they have to do.

5. Blue: People on a 5 Life Path need to make constructive use of freedom. They are versatile, capable peo-

ple who enjoy change and variety. Once they find the correct field for them, they can make great progress.

6. Indigo: People on a 6 Life Path need to learn how to handle responsibility. They are caring, loving people who enjoy helping others, and frequently take up careers in the service industries. They have good taste and are often highly creative.

7. Violet: People on a 7 Life Path need to grow in knowledge and wisdom. They are intuitive, spiritual people who enjoy spending time on their own to think, meditate, and understand.

8. Pink: People on an 8 Life Path need to learn how to handle the pressures and pleasures of the material world. They are ambitious, practical people who generally strive for success, enjoying the status and rewards that follow as a result.

9. Bronze: People on a 9 Life Path must learn the pleasures of giving. They are tolerant, sympathetic, idealistic humanitarians who give to others in many different ways. Along with 3 and 6, 9 is a number with creative potential.

Eleven and 22 are known as Master Numbers in numerology. This is because people with a Master Number in their makeup are capable of achieving more than most. However, it usually takes a large part of their lives before they can make constructive use of their potential. There is always a degree of nervous tension associated with a Master Number, and this holds them back in the early parts of their lives. Consequently, it usually takes several incarnations before these people fulfill their true potential.

11. Silver: People on an 11 Life Path possess special awarenesses and perceptions that are not available to most people. They are intuitive, spiritual daydreamers who are good at coming up with ideas and making plans, but seldom follow through with them.

22. Gold: People on a 22 Life Path have the potential to achieve anything they set their minds on. They are practical, charismatic, and inspirational. However, their problem is learning how to handle and focus all of the power at their disposal. They need to learn how to use their gifts to help mankind as a whole.

The color determined by your Life Path number cannot be changed, as your date of birth is fixed. You may or may not like this color, but it is yours for life.

There is one other color that cannot be changed, either. This is the color determined by the day of the month you were born in, reduced down to a single digit (except, of course, if you were born on the 11th, 22nd, or 29th of any month).

Your Expression Number

The two other important numbers in numerology are your Expression and Soul Urge numbers. These are both derived from your full name at birth. The Expression number reveals your natural abilities, and your Soul Urge reveals your inner desires.

To determine these numbers, you need to convert the letters in your full name at birth into numbers, and then reduce them down to a single digit (or an 11 or 22). This is done using the following chart:

1	2	3	4	5	6	7	8	9
A	B	C	D	E	F	G	H	I
J	K	L	M	N	O	P	Q	R
S	T	U	V	W	X	Y	Z	

Here is an example of someone called Bradley Sebastian Smith:

```
BRADLEY    SEBASTIAN    SMITH
2914357    152112915    14928
   31          27          24
    4           9           6
```

$4 + 9 + 6 = 19$, and $1 + 9 = 10$, and $1 + 0 = 1$. Bradley has an Expression number of 1.

If you look at the interpretation for 1 in the chart above, you will see that Bradley is naturally independent, enthusiastic and ambitious. The color relating to number 1 is red, which means that red plays an important part in Bradley's life.

The Soul Urge

The Soul Urge is derived from the vowels in Bradley's name, again reduced down to a single digit (except, of course, if they reduce down to an 11 or 22). The letter "Y" is sometimes considered a vowel in numerology. If it is not pronounced, or forms part of a vowel, it is considered to be a vowel, which means that it is included when working out the Soul Urge number. Bradley has a "Y" in his name, but it is not pronounced. Consequently, it is classified as a vowel. The "Y" in the name Yolande is pronounced, and therefore is not counted when working out the Soul Urge number. I have come across a number of surnames over the years that contain two "Y's," one of which is included in the Soul Urge, while the other is not. "Yancey" and "Yockney" are two examples.

Here is how we work out Bradley's Soul Urge number:

```
BRADLEY  SEBASTIAN  SMITH
1      57   5 1   91      9
    13          16        9
    4           7         9
```

$4 + 7 + 9 = 20$, and $2 + 0 = 2$. Bradley's Soul Urge number is 2. This means that Bradley enjoys getting on with people, and being tactful and diplomatic. His Soul Urge color is orange.

Day of Birth

Let's give Bradley a date of birth to complete his picture. Let's assume he was born on August 4, 1975. This means he has a Life Path number of 7. Consequently, Bradley's numbers and colors are:

Life Path 7 Violet

Expression 1 Red

Soul Urge 2 Orange

Day of Birth 4 Green

All of these colors will be important to Bradley as he goes through life. If he is working on something that plays a major role in his life, he should use violet. If he wants to be good at something, he should use red. If he wants to make something more enjoyable, orange would be a good color for him to use. He can use green at any time. Any, and all, of these colors will prove stimulating and invigorating to him, as they are all part of his makeup.

However, Bradley is unlikely to be known by his full name to everyone. His friends might call him Brad, while his parents call him Bradley. He might sign his name "Bradley S. Smith." Any changes of this sort are likely to affect his Expression and Soul Urge numbers, which then alters the colors. As Brad Smith, he has an Expression of 4 and a Soul Urge of 1. This increases the amount of green he is reflecting, but at the same time eliminates the orange. This is not entirely bad, however, as the colors from his full name at birth never entirely disappear. In numerology, it is believed that everybody chooses their own name at birth to receive the experiences they need to learn in this incarnation. Consequently, no matter how many times Bradley changes his name, the basic colors will always be there.

Your Personal Colors

Bradley S. Smith gives him an Expression number of 2 and a Soul Urge of 1. This is an excellent name for him to use, as none of the colors change.

In fact, very few people are limited to four colors, as the individual letters of the person's full name at birth provide additional colors. Let's look at Bradley's name again.

BRADLEY   SEBASTIAN   SMITH
2 9 1 4 3 5 7   1 5 2 1 1 2 9 1 5   1 4 9 2 8

If you look at all the numbers below the letters of his name, you will see that he has all the letters from 1 to 9, except for number 6, which relates to indigo. This means that Bradley would benefit by adding the color indigo to his life. He might wear something that is indigo in color. Alternatively, he might include indigo in his breathing exercises. By doing this, he would subconsciously feel more whole and complete.

Bradley is missing just one color. Some people have names that include every color, while other people are missing three, four, or even more colors. Here's an example:

WENDY   FOX
5 5 5 4 7   6 6 6

Wendy is missing: 1 (red), 2 (orange), 3 (yellow), 8 (pink) and 9 (bronze). Of course, she is not missing all of them, as she has an 8 Expression number and a 9 Soul Urge. Wendy's life would improve immensely if she started absorbing her missing colors (red, orange, and yellow).

You can take this even further by looking at the relative quantities of each number in your full name at birth. Ideally,

57

you want a balance. If one or two colors are overemphasized at the expense of the others, you are likely to be using their qualities negatively, rather than positively. This also applies, but in a slightly different way, if the color is absent. These are all lessons that need to be learned as you progress through life. Frequently, people make the same mistake over and over again until they finally learn the lesson that the color is teaching them.

It is not easy to determine if a color is in balance. Here is an approximation that will help you work out your own name. If your full name at birth contains eighteen letters, the ideal ratings of colors would be:

Red 3

Orange 2

Yellow 2

Green 2

Blue 2

Indigo 2

Violet 1

Pink 2

Bronze 2

Here are the meanings for each color in your full name at birth:

Red

If red is in balance, you are confident, self-assured, and able to initiate projects. You can rely on yourself.

If red is absent or low, you will lack confidence and the ability to start new projects. You will find it hard to be independent.

If red is high compared to the other colors, you are likely to be aggressive, and force your own needs and desires onto others.

Orange

If orange is in balance, you will work well with others. You will be cooperative and diplomatic when necessary. You will be open, honest, and self-assured.

If orange is absent or low, you will be oversensitive and find it hard to cooperate easily with others.

If orange is high compared to the other colors, you will be highly emotional and overly reliant on others.

Yellow

If yellow is in balance, you will be outgoing and sociable, and express yourself well. You might have a desire to express yourself creatively.

If yellow is absent or low, you will find it hard to express yourself, and will be retiring, even shy, in nature. You will be anxious and lack enthusiasm.

If yellow is high compared to the other colors, you will be frivolous, boastful, and superficial. You will invariably put pleasure ahead of work.

Green

If green is in balance, you will be able to work hard, when necessary, and will pay attention to details.

If green is absent or low, you will try to avoid hard work and are likely to be indecisive and careless with details.

If green is high compared to the other colors, you will become so immersed in the details and minutiae that you will fail to see the overall picture.

Blue

If blue is in balance, you will enjoy change and variety. You will be generous, easy to get on with, and will use your personal freedom responsibly.

If blue is absent or low, you will find it hard to accept change, and will be lacking in trust and ambition.

If blue is high compared to the other colors, you will be inclined to overindulge, and will frequently make changes for no apparent reason.

Indigo

If indigo is in balance, you will be able to accept and handle responsibility. You will gain enormous pleasure from helping others.

If indigo is absent or low, you will find it hard to accept responsibility, but will expect perfection from others. You will find it hard to trust others.

If indigo is high compared to the other colors, you will be involved in family and domestic matters to the exclusion of virtually everything else.

Violet

If violet is in balance, you will be understanding, compassionate, analytical, and have an interest in spirituality.

If violet is absent or low, you will be impatient, and have little interest in organized religion. You are likely to build up a faith of your own.

If violet is high compared to the other colors, you will search for wisdom, knowledge, and truth. It is rare for anyone to have a high rating of violet.

Pink

If pink is in balance, you will be involved in the material world, but have a sense of proportion and possess a healthy self-esteem. You will be able to put your ideas into action.

If pink is absent or low, you will find it hard to appreciate the true value of the material world, and are likely to strive for possessions and other signs of worldly success. You are likely to lack self-esteem.

If pink is high compared to the other colors, you will be motivated solely by power, money, and worldly success.

You will feel superior to people who have not achieved the same level of material success as you.

Bronze

If bronze is in balance, you will be concerned for humanity in general.

If bronze is low or absent, you will be lacking in compassion and concern for humanity in general. It is rare for anyone to be deficient in bronze.

If bronze is high compared to the other colors, you will be rigid, stubborn and determined to do things your way. You will have a slightly detached concern for humanity in general.

Hidden Desire

Your hidden desire is determined by looking at all the colors in your full name at birth and determining which has the highest number attached to it. As most people have more "blues" than any other color, you need to subtract two from the number in the blues column before determining this.

Let's look at Wendy Fox again:

WENDY   FOX
5 5 5 4 7   6 66

    Red 0
    Orange 0
    Yellow 0
    Green 1

Blue 3
Indigo 3
Violet 1
Pink 0
Bronze 0

The two highest rating colors in Wendy's name are blue and indigo. However, we need to subtract two from the blue, which leaves it with a 1. Consequently, indigo represents Wendy's Hidden Desire.

Here is another example:

HAMI SH   DONAL D   S IMMER TON
8 1 4 9 1 8   4 6 5 1 3 4   1 94 4 5 9 26 5

Red 4
Orange 1
Yellow 1
Green 5
Blue 3
Indigo 2
Violet 0
Pink 2
Bronze 3

Hamish's Hidden Desire is green.

Here is an example of someone with two Hidden Desires:

S I MONE   PAUL I NE   S MI TH
1 9 4 6 5 5   7 1 3 3 9 5 5   1 4 9 2 8

Red 3
Orange 1

Yellow 2

Green 2

Blue 4

Indigo 1

Violet 1

Pink 1

Bronze 3

We need to subtract two from Simone's highest rating color, blue. This leaves red and bronze as her highest rating colors, and this means she has two Hidden Desires.

Interpretations of the Hidden Desires

- Red: A desire for independence, leadership, and attainment.

- Orange: A desire for cooperation, harmony, and association.

- Yellow: A desire for creative self-expression.

- Green: A desire for constructive, detailed work.

- Blue: A desire for freedom, variety, and change.

- Indigo: A desire for home, family, responsibility, and reputation.

- Violet: A desire for wisdom, knowledge, and hidden truths.

- Pink: A desire for material success.

- Bronze: A desire for universal love and knowledge.

Color of the Day

You can use the formula for determining someone's Life Path to determine your color for any specific day. Try wearing a little of the color of the day for a month or so and see what effects each color has on you. This is an excellent way to experiment with the power, feelings, and potential that different colors have on you.

If you are naturally the life and soul of every occasion, you might find yourself quieter and more contemplative on violet days. Conversely, if you are normally quiet and retiring, you might find yourself more extroverted on red days.

After doing this for a while, you may choose to make some changes in your wardrobe to help you become the person you want to be. There is nothing false or artificial about this. If you are a shy, retiring person, it is a good idea to boost your confidence with a bit of red or orange. If your work is mentally challenging, you might want to wear some yellow to enhance your intellect. By doing this, you are helping yourself become the person you want to be.

Your personal colors reveal a great deal about you, but cannot provide the complete picture. This is because all the colors of the rainbow are present in your aura. Fortunately, the ability to feel and see auras is a skill that anyone can learn. That is the topic of the next chapter.

CHAPTER FOUR

YOU ARE A RAINBOW

An invisible energy field known as the aura surrounds all living things. People who see auras are able to use it to determine people's character, moods, and state of health. Auras reveal the state of our physical, mental, and spiritual health. The word *aura* comes from the Greek word *avra*, which means a "breeze." A Russian couple, Semyon and Valentina Kirlian, were the first to photograph auras, proving the existence of something that clairvoyant people have known about for thousands of years.

The aura is not something that surrounds the physical body. It is actually an extension of the body. Some people see it the other way around and feel that the physical body is created by the energy field, which in turn is created by our consciousness. Kirlian photography demonstrates there is something to be said for this argument. If you take a Kirlian photograph of your hand while thinking about something that makes you angry, you will produce a completely different photograph to the one you'll take if you think about someone you love.

The size of the aura depends on the spiritual development of the person, and also on his or her level of energy. Buddha is believed to have had an aura that extended for fifty miles. Auras also expand in the sunlight and contract when indoors. They shrink even more in total darkness, but never entirely disappear.

The Chakras

The aura connects with the physical body through seven energy centers known as chakras, which are centers of power located in the aura alongside the spinal column. *Chakra* is a Sanskrit word that means "wheel." This is the perfect name, as psychics see the chakras as revolving discs of energy. Each chakra relates to a different color of the rainbow, which is why I called this chapter "You Are a Rainbow." You, and every other person in the world, contain all of the colors of the rainbow inside your aura.

How to Feel Auras

Some people see auras naturally, but it is a skill that anyone can develop. It is usually better to start feeling for auras.

Once you can do that, you will find it easier to develop your auric sight.

Start by relaxing comfortably for a few minutes. When you feel ready, rub your hands together briskly for several seconds and then hold them about twelve inches apart. You may feel some energy between the two hands, especially in the center of the palms and in the fingertips. Slowly bring your hands together. At some stage you will feel a slight resistance as the auras from each hand meet. To me, it feels like a soft, squashy ball. You may experience it in a different way. My students have come up with many descriptions over the years. Usually, they notice a slight resistance, a tingling sensation, or a feeling of warmth. Some people experience the opposite, and feel a sense of coolness.

Once you have felt the auras meet, continue to bring your hands together. You will notice the feeling of resistance disappear as the auras from each hand merge into each other. Hold your hands together for a few seconds and then slowly draw them apart again. You will notice a slight sense of coolness on your palms and fingertips as the auras separate again.

You can experiment with this by bringing your hands together until you feel the aura, then moving them apart again, and noticing the coolness.

How to Feel Chakras

Once you can do this, you can experiment further by feeling your chakras. As the chakras are, in effect, batteries, your personal electromagnetic energy is stronger at these points and you will be able to feel them with your hands. Once you have done this, you'll wonder why you never noticed this additional energy before.

The seven chakras are aligned along the spinal column in the etheric body:

1. The Root chakra is situated at the base of the spine.

2. The Sacral chakra is situated halfway between your pubic bone and navel.

3. The Solar chakra is situated at the level of your solar plexus.

4. The Heart chakra is situated between the shoulder blades in line with your heart.

5. The Throat chakra is situated at the level of the throat.

6. The Brow chakra is situated at the level of your forehead, slightly above your eyebrows.

7. The Crown chakra is situated at the top of your head.

You will have felt at least some of your chakras respond involuntarily in the past. When you were overcome with emotion, you may have felt something in your heart. This is your heart chakra. Your throat chakra is responsible for the choked-up feeling you experience when you can't speak.

The heart chakra is the easiest one to feel. Again, hold your hand about twelve inches away from your chest, and slowly bring it closer and closer. Pause when you feel a slight resistance. Draw your hand away until the resistance goes, and then bring it forward again to experience the sense of resistance again. Once you are certain that you have felt your heart chakra you can start feeling it for size and shape. You will find that it is shaped like a cone or trumpet, and it will feel surprisingly solid. Once you have examined your heart chakra, you can start feeling for the others.

Working with a Partner

Your progress at feeling auras will progress more quickly if you have a like-minded partner to experiment with. A friend with similar interests is usually a better choice than a family member. This is because family members will be doing it out of a sense of obligation, rather than because they want to.

Ask your friend to sit comfortably in a chair. Stand behind him or her and hold your hands about twelve inches from each side of your friend's head. Slowly bring your hands closer to your friend's head until you feel a resistance. Test it by moving your hands away and back again. Frequently, your friend will feel the sensation in his or her aura as soon as you touch it.

Once you have found your friend's aura, move your hands in different directions to see if you can trace the aura all the way around his or her body. After this, it is time to swap places, so that your friend can make the same discoveries that you have.

Once you have both felt each other's auras, you can feel for the chakras. Ask your friend to lie down on a bed, and close his eyes. Your friend can lie on his or her back or stomach, but you will find it easier to experiment with the person lying on his or her back. It is also easier if your friend takes off any heavy clothing first.

Your friend will not be able to see what you are doing, but will usually be able to tell you when you are feeling one of the chakras. This will provide dramatic evidence for both of you that you are on the right track.

Everything you have done so far is designed to help you gain more awareness of your aura, and auras in general. You may even have clairvoyantly determined your friend's aura colors while feeling them. However, the next experiments will help you to see them.

How to See Auras

The first experiment is to place your forefingers together and gaze at them for about ten seconds. Then slowly move them apart. You will notice a fine, barely detectable, thread of energy that keeps the fingertips connected, even though you are slowly moving them apart. The first time you do this the thread is likely to disappear once your fingers are about half an inch apart. However, with practice, you will find that you can move your fingers further and further apart and still see the thin line of energy. If you have any difficulty in doing this, try dimming the lights and hold your fingers over a sheet of white paper. This works well for most people, but a few of my students preferred a darker background. Experiment and see which works better for you.

Once you can do this successfully, you can try putting all four fingertips together and see the threads of energy that join each finger. If you are doing this with a partner, see if you can see the threads of energy between his or her fingertips.

It is also interesting to place your fingertips in contact with your friend's and see what happens. As you are friends, you will see the thin lines of energy as you move your fingers away.

The next experiment also uses your hands. You will need a plain-colored wall and dimmed lighting. Stand several feet away from the wall, facing it. Extend your right hand out in front of you, with your fingers spread and facing the ceiling. Look at the wall through your fingers. Focus on the wall, rather than your fingers. After a few moments, you will notice that your hand has a distinct aura around it. You will probably see it as an almost invisible gray haze. When you become aware of this, focus on the aura. You may find that it disappears as soon as you do this. If this happens, gaze at the wall again until it returns. You may have to do this several times before you can look at the aura without having it disappear. Once you are able to do this, look at your fingertips. You may see fine streams of energy radiating outwards from the tips of your fingers. You may notice that your entire aura is constantly moving.

Once you can clearly see the aura surrounding your right hand, repeat the exercise with your left hand, and other parts of your body. As it is easier to see the aura around naked flesh than around clothing, you might like to experiment naked or partially clothed.

Many people are disappointed when they first see their auras, as they expect to see glorious colors. These will gradually appear as your auric sight develops. Most people start by seeing the aura as almost colorless, but over a period of time, your color awareness will develop.

Now that you can see your own aura, you should experiment with your partner. Have him or her stand a few feet in front of a plain-colored wall. Stand several steps away and look in the direction of your friend, but focus on the wall behind him or her. You should notice your friend's aura in the same way you saw the aura around your hand. There is no need to try hard. Simply focus on the wall, and allow your friend's aura to reveal itself to you.

You may notice a hazy aura that entirely surrounds your friend. You may see it around his or her head and neck, and not see anything anywhere else. This is because clothing restricts the aura, making it harder to see.

Once you see your friend's aura, focus on it. It may disappear when you do this. Simply focus on the wall again until you can see it again, and then try once more. Keep on doing this until you can examine the aura in detail. You will notice how it shimmers and moves. Once you see it clearly, move forward and touch it. The chances are that the aura will disappear as soon as you do this. If this occurs, go back to your previous position, and wait for the aura to reappear, and then try again. When you finally touch it, it will feel the same as it did before you could see it. However, now you will be able to notice the resistance when you press on it, and observe how increased pressure allows you to move inside the aura.

Feel the aura in different parts of your friend's body. Pay particular attention to the chakras, and notice how they rapidly rotate. As mentioned earlier, this is why they are called chakras, from the Sanskrit word that means "wheel."

Now that you can see the aura, you can perform some experiments. Ask your friend to think of something that makes him or her angry, and notice any changes in the aura. The aura might shrink or take on a dirty red hue. Follow this up by asking your friend to think of happy and sad events, and observe what occurs.

Another interesting experiment is to visit a busy environment, such as a shopping mall. Walk several paces behind your friend and see if you can see his or her aura in that type of situation. You will find this much more difficult. However, after you have succeeded at this, you will also start noticing auras around other people.

Practice as much as you can. Everyone is different. Some people find it a simple matter to see auras, but others find it takes time. Be patient if it takes you longer than you expected. The important thing is to have fun with your practice. A playful, lighthearted approach works much better than grim determination. Try experimenting in different environments and under different lighting conditions. In time, you will be able to see auras whenever you wish.

You will find your ability to see auras an extremely useful skill. You'll be able to determine people's moods, for instance, by looking at their auras. You'll often know when someone is lying. However, nothing could be more important than health. Health matters are often visible in the aura long before the person is aware of any problem. That is the subject of the next chapter.

CHAPTER FIVE

COLOR HEALING

Archaeologists have discovered special rooms in ancient Egyptian temples in which the sun's rays were broken up to form rainbows. Patients would sit in rooms that corresponded to the specific color they needed.[1] Consequently, the basic principles of color healing have been known for thousands of years.

Color healing has been practiced for thousands of years in India, also. They worked on the aura and the chakras. In the *Kurma Purana*, one of the sacred texts of the Hindus, the creator of the world is referred to as "Grandfather." He is visualized as millions of colored rays that reach every part of the universe, providing light and life.

Chinese medicine has used color to promote healing for thousands of years.

The ancient Greeks studied color healing, and the basic ideas formulated by Pythagoras and Hippocrates remained unchallenged in the West until the Middle Ages.

Avicenna (980–c.1037), an Arab physician, wrote a book called *Canon of Medicine* that described his system of color therapy. He prescribed potions made from red flowers to people with blood disorders, and yellow flowers for people who had problems with their bile duct.

During the Renaissance, Theophrastus Bombastus von Hohenheim (1493–1541), better known as Paracelsus, used light and color extensively in his medical practice.

However, the emphasis of medicine gradually changed. By the nineteenth century, doctors were treating the physical body and ignoring the mental and spiritual aspects of their patients.

Color healing went into a decline until the 1870s, when three valuable books were published in America. The first of these was *Blue and Sun-lights* by Augustus Pleasanton, which appeared in 1876. He claimed to have healed animals and people by exposing them to blue light. Although this book proved popular, the medical establishment ignored it. However, just one year later, an eminent physician named Dr. Seth Pancoast published his book, *Blue and Red Lights*, which endorsed the principles of color healing.

In 1878, Edwin S. Babbitt produced his monumental work, *The Principles of Light and Color*. This book was hugely successful. It upset the medical fraternity, but the general public considered Edwin Babbitt a miracle worker. Different schools of color therapy developed as a result of this book, and some of them are still active today. Edwin Babbitt considered red, blue, and yellow to be the main healing colors. He thought each color had a complementary color that could be used to restore the patient to vibrant health. If someone was overly hostile or aggressive, for instance, he would prescribe them several sessions under a green light to calm them down. This is because green is the complementary color to red, and the negative traits of red include aggression.

Arguably, Edwin Babbitt could claim to be the father of modern-day color healing. His book is still readily available, and the influence he has had on later generations of color healers is immeasurable.

The next major influence was a Hindu scientist, Colonel Dinshah P. Ghadiali, who published his major work, *Spectro-Chrome Metry Encyclopedia*, in 1933.[2] Colonel Ghadiali discovered that every organ of the body could be either stimulated or inhibited by a specific color. Obviously, if you know the organ that is affected and the color that will bring it back into balance, you will be able to effect a healing.

Today, research into the subject is continuing, and organizations such as the International Association of Colour are ensuring that practitioners are receiving proper training and education.[3] Although it is still a controversial subject, color healing is once again coming into its own as a valuable means of healing the body, mind, and spirit.

The basic principle behind color therapy is that energies can be stimulated in different parts of the body by exposure to particular colors, and this enables healing to occur. Some of the longstanding beliefs of color healers are now being confirmed by science. Dr. Robert Gerard, a Los Angeles psychologist, studied the effects that color had on human physiology. In his paper on the subject he wrote that blood pressure, respiration rate, eye blinks, and brain wave patterns increased when a person was exposed to red, but decreased when a person was exposed to blue.[4]

Most color healing is done through the aura, particularly the chakras. Although the chakras are aspects of consciousness, they still have a major influence over physical functioning.

When someone is healthy in mind, body, and spirit, his or her aura will literally glow with vitality and energy. However, any dis-ease in these three areas is revealed clearly inside the aura. Accidents cannot always be averted, but apart from these, most ill health is caused by years of negative thinking. This is apparent in the aura long before it is revealed in the physical body. Our mental and emotional states constantly affect our auras for better or worse. Interestingly, the auras of color healers also change when they are performing healing on others. It was reported that the aura of a spiritual healer called Ethel de Loach changed the instant she began her healing sessions. The blue streams of light that surrounded her hands normally changed into a vivid orange glow.[5]

Over the years, researchers have discovered the healing properties of different colors.

Red

Red is stimulating and exciting. It revitalizes the entire body. It activates the blood and the senses. Consequently, it can be used with problems concerning sight, sound, smell, taste, and touch. It is also good for muscular problems and the liver.

Illnesses that respond well to red include: anaemia, asthma, bronchitis, colds (as long as there is no fever), circulation problems, constipation, depression, endocrine gland problems, paralysis, pneumonia, reproductive problems, tuberculosis, and varicose veins.

Orange

Orange stimulates the metabolism, digestion, sexual energy, and athletic performance. It creates feelings of wellbeing and contentment.

Illnesses that respond well to orange include: asthma, bladder problems, bronchitis, chronic exhaustion, colds, depression, elimination problems, epilepsy, kidney ailments, lung problems, rheumatism, tumors, and urinary problems.

Yellow

Yellow provides energy for the muscular system, the nervous system and the brain. It stimulates and purifies the blood and lymph systems. It cleanses the liver, intestines, and the skin. It has a psychological effect on the body, creating feelings of cheerfulness and positivity.

Illnesses that respond well to yellow include: constipation, diabetes, dyspepsia, eczema, flatulence, indigestion, kidney problems, paralysis, piles, rheumatism, and the spleen.

Green

Green stimulates growth of the bones and muscles. It releases tension and is emotionally soothing. It is calming, and promotes peace and restfulness. Green is a natural tonic.

Illnesses that respond well to green include: asthma, backache, colic, hay fever, headaches, head colds, heart conditions, high blood pressure, laryngitis, malaria, neuralgia, piles, typhoid, ulcers, and venereal diseases.

Blue

Blue has a cooling effect that helps inflamed organs return to balance. It soothes emotional problems and relaxes the mind.

Illnesses that respond well to blue include: apoplexy, biliousness, bowel problems, burns, cataracts, chicken pox, colic, duodenal ulcers, dysentery, epilepsy, fevers, gastrointestinal problems, goiters, headaches, insomnia, jaundice, laryngitis, measles, polio, rashes, renal problems, rheumatism, and sore throats.

Indigo

Indigo is cooling and acts as an astringent. It also purifies the bloodstream.

Illnesses that respond well to indigo include: appendicitis, asthma, bronchitis, cataracts, dyspepsia, ear problems (including deafness), eye problems, hyperthyroidism, lung problems, nervous conditions, nosebleeds, palsy, pneumonia, throat problems, tonsillitis, and whooping cough.

Violet

Violet nourishes and purifies the blood. It stimulates the spleen, and is good for bone growth.

Illnesses that respond well to violet include: bladder problems, concussion, cramps, epilepsy, insomnia, kidney problems, neuralgia, nervous disorders, rheumatism, sciatica, skin problems, and tumors.

Diagnosis is done in a variety of ways. Color therapists who can see auras are able to determine what is wrong with a patient by examining his or her aura. Frequently, a pendulum is used to determine what colors would be the most beneficial for the patient.

Color is administered to the patient in a variety of ways. Color healers frequently shine lights of the colors that the patient requires on the area that needs attention. These lights contain special quartz filters to produce colors of varying wavelengths and frequencies.

Different colored oils and flower essences are used as well. Dr. Edward Bach, the British physician who created a form of healing using flower essences, arranged his floral remedies into seven groups, each of which was associated with a different color.

Water is sometimes poured into glasses of different colors and then exposed to light for four hours. This treated water will last for up to two weeks in a refrigerator. The patient receives the benefit of the color when he or she drinks the water.

Crystals of different colors are sometimes placed on the patients' bodies to help healing. Patients may be advised to wear clothing of certain colors to aid the healing process.

It is possible to stimulate colors that are deficient, or lacking, in the aura by eating foods of the right color. Red can be obtained from meat, beets, peppers, grapes, and red-skinned fruit. Orange can be obtained from oranges, carrots, pumpkins, sweet corn, and apricots. Yellow can be obtained from butter, egg yolks, grapefruit, melons, and yellow-skinned fruits and vegetables. Green can be obtained from green vegetables and fruits. Blue can be obtained from blueberries and plums. Indigo can be obtained from grapes, plums, blueberries, and blackberries. Violet can be obtained from beets, eggplants, grapes, blackberries, and purple broccoli and asparagus.

Some healers use visualization to send specific colors to their patients. This is the method that Swami Panchadasi used almost one hundred years ago. He describes the process in his book *The Human Aura*: "A nervous, unstrung patient may be treated by bathing him mentally in a flood of violet or lavender auric color; while a tired, used up, fatigued person may be invigorated by flooding him with bright reds, followed by bright, rich yellows, finishing the treatment with a steady flow of warm orange color." The session concludes by visualizing the patient surrounded by a great white light. "This will leave the patient in an inspired, exalted, illuminated state of mind and soul, which will be of great benefit to him, and will also have the effect of reinvigorating the healer by cosmic energy."[6]

Of course, you can also do this yourself, whenever necessary. If you are feeling exhausted, visualize yourself breathing in the color red. If you are suffering from stress or find it hard to relax, breathe in green. Ideally, color breathing should be performed before or after breakfast. If this is not possible, the next best time is before or immediately after the evening meal.

If you are breathing in the first three colors (red, orange, and yellow), you should visualize them flowing into your body from the earth. Green should be visualized as flowing horizontally into the solar plexus. The final three (blue, indigo and violet) should be visualized as flowing into your body from the top of your head.

Healing Through the Chakras

Many illnesses are caused when the person blocks off his or her feelings as a response to unpleasant experiences. As a result of this, the functioning of the affected chakra is reduced or even totally blocked. This means that the color and emotions that relate to that particular chakra are sent back out into the world, instead of being absorbed. Consequently, someone who has closed off his root chakra (red) will project his anger and rage onto others and "see red." Someone who closes off his throat chakra (blue) will cease communicating effectively and will seem "blue."

Root Chakra—Red

The root chakra is concerned with security and survival. It grounds us to the earth. When this chakra is healthy and balanced, the person feels secure. This chakra is also related to the mother. Someone who feels separated from his or her mother will lack a sense of security. Tension and stress also create insecurity and a threat to survival.

The root chakra looks after the legs, the skeleton, and the elimination system. Consequently, problems in these areas may be a result of tension in the root chakra.

Any exercise that uses the legs, such as walking, running, or jumping, stimulates the root chakra. You can also stimulate it by sitting in a straight-backed chair with your feet flat on the floor. If you push down into the floor with your legs you will stimulate your root chakra.

Sacral Chakra—Orange

The sacral chakra is concerned with pleasure. It is responsible for the lower back and the organs in the lower abdomen (large intestine, the bladder, and the reproductive system). It looks after the fluidic system of the body, and also relates to our sense of taste.

People who find it hard to express their emotions experience problems such as lower back pain, constipation, impotence, painful or irregular menstruation, and arthritis. People who are repressed or experiencing emotional pain are likely to have blocked sacral chakras. Conversely, people who are oversensitive or emotionally dependent on others are also likely to experience problems with this chakra.

All pleasurable activities stimulate the sacral chakra. If you are not experiencing fun in your life, your sacral chakra may be out of balance. You would benefit by doing anything that provides you with a sense of pleasure, satisfaction, or happiness. All creative activities stimulate this chakra.

Solar Plexus Chakra—Yellow

When the solar plexus chakra is working efficiently, you feel good about yourself and who you are. It is your seat of personal power. If your personal power is threatened or taken away, you are likely to experience problems with the areas looked after by this chakra. Feelings of guilt and shame are common ways of depleting personal power.

The solar plexus chakra looks after the muscular system, eyesight, the skin, and the organs close to it, such as the stomach and gall bladder.

Spending time in the sunlight stimulates the solar plexus chakra. Thinking positive and supportive thoughts about yourself helps raise your self-esteem and stimulates your solar plexus chakra.

Heart Chakra—Green

Not surprisingly, the heart chakra is concerned with feelings of love and your relationships with the people who are closest to you.

The heart chakra is concerned with the well-being of your heart, lungs, immune system and the circulation of blood throughout the body. When the heart chakra is well balanced you will accept yourself and other people for who they are. You will be understanding, tolerant, and not likely to feel threatened by insecure people who try to control everything around them.

When you feel insecure, unloved, or unlovable, you may experience breathing problems (as this chakra is associated with the element of Air) or have difficulties with your immune system.

Thinking about the special people in your life is an effective way to stimulate the heart chakra. A policy of being compassionate and gentle with everyone you meet also helps energize your heart chakra. Walking in a park with plenty of greenery also stimulates the heart chakra.

Throat Chakra—Blue

The throat chakra is concerned with communication and creativity. It relates to the arms, shoulders, neck, and thyroid gland. It is also involved with your sense of hearing.

When the throat chakra is well balanced you will feel contented and at peace. You will listen to what others have to say, and feel able to freely express your own views.

Singing, dancing, or playing a musical instrument are effective ways to stimulate the throat chakra. Any form of self-expression, such as repeating mantras or affirmations, stimulates the throat chakra.

Brow Chakra—Indigo

The brow chakra is concerned with thinking, perception, spirituality and extrasensory perception. It is situated in the area known as the third eye. It controls the endocrine system and is also involved, with the chakras immediately above and below it, with the senses of sight and hearing.

When the brow chakra is well balanced you will be able to "see" clearly. This relates to your vision, but also includes your ability to perceive or understand, the whole picture. This perception includes your intuition so that you will feel able to act on your hunches.

When the brow chakra is out of balance you are likely to experience headaches and eye problems. You will also find it hard to maintain a sense of perspective.

The brow chakra can be stimulated by deliberately spending time away from your problems.

Crown Chakra—Violet

The crown chakra is our connection with the divine. The root chakra connects us with earth, while the crown chakra gives us a link to heaven. Also, as the root chakra is connected with the mother, the crown chakra is related to the father. Someone who is separated from his or her father is likely to experience a sense of isolation. This also makes it hard for the person to establish a connection with God.

The brow chakra is concerned with the pineal gland, the brain, and the nervous system. It is also related to coordination and a sense of direction.

When the brow chakra is out of balance you are likely to avoid responsibility, and feel lonely and isolated, even with other people around you.

The crown chakra can be stimulated by meditation, and by setting worthwhile goals. Any activities relating to your faith or philosophy of life will also stimulate your crown chakra.

Crystals and Gemstones for the Chakras

Crystals and gemstones that relate to the colors of the specific chakras are frequently used for healing purposes. They should be placed on the area of the specific chakra for about twenty minutes a day. Gemstones for the crown chakra are usually placed on the floor or bed directly above the head of the patient.

Crystals and gemstones that can be used include:

- Root Chakra: Bloodstone, Coral, Diamond, Garnet, Heliotrope, Jade, Red Jasper, Rose Quartz, Ruby (Hematite and Obsidian can also be used)
- Sacral Chakra: Carnelian, Citrine, Fire Opal, Orange Agate, Pearl, Rhodolite, Ruby, Zincite
- Solar Plexus Chakra: Amber, Citrine, Honey Calcite, Peach Aventurine, Tiger-eye, Gold Topaz
- Heart Chakra: Aventurine, Chrysoprase, Emerald, Green Calcite, Malachite, Moss Agate, Peridot
- Throat Chakra: Amazonite, Aquamarine, Blue Lace Agate, Chalcedony, Chrysocolla, Blue Topaz, Blue Tourmaline
- Brow Chakra: Azurite, Emerald, Fluorite, Howlite, Iolite, Lapis Lazuli, Luvulite, Sapphire, Sodalite
- Crown Chakra: Amethyst, Clear Quartz, Diamond, Fluorite, Gold Calcite, Rutilated Quartz, Spinel, Tourmaline

If the specific gemstones are not available, rock crystal and rutillated quartz can be used. Crystals and gemstones can also be used to provide a protective shield when performing healing work. I place several green gemstones on the floor to surround the area I will be working in. Any crystals or gemstones can be used. I like green for this purpose as it relates to healing. Crystals and gemstones are covered in more detail in chapter twelve.

Color therapy should be used only as an adjunct to whatever your medical doctor advises. Your doctor should always be your first health professional, as he or she has undergone years of study and training. Be careful when selecting a color therapist. Ethical color therapists are cautious in their claims. Be wary of anyone who claims they can use color therapy to heal someone at a distance, or who claims instant healings. Absent, or distant, healing can be done by spiritual healers, but this does not usually include sending color to the person. Instant healings can occur, but usually color therapy takes time. Color therapy will not cure any illness caused by a deficiency in the system.

When you think of the influence color has on us, it's not surprising it plays such an important role in health. However, I have met people who accept the role of color in healing but are amazed to discover colors can reveal so much about their personalities. They find it hard to believe that naming liked and disliked colors can provide so much information. We'll look at this aspect of color psychology in the next chapter.

CHAPTER SIX

WHAT YOUR
FAVORITE COLOR REVEALS

What is your favorite color today? Strange as it may seem, your favorite color today may be different from your favorite color last year, last week, or even yesterday. Children change their favorite colors frequently, but adults also change their favorite color from time to time, and this reflects what is going on in their lives.

Every color can be interpreted. Unfortunately, there is not enough space to describe every possible color. Also, there are slight differences in meaning between different shadings of the same color. Lime green is different from dark green, but for the purposes of this exercise they are both "green." If your favorite color is not included here, choose the color that is closest to the one you like.

Some people say they do not have a favorite color, as they like every color. If you fit into this category, for the purposes of this exercise, choose the color that inspires you.

Red

Red is the most popular color for many people, especially extroverts. However, it can also be the favorite color of people who are seeking to become more extroverted. If red is your favorite color you are outgoing, ambitious, and hard-working. You enjoy competition, physical activities, and achieving your goals. You have a sense of the dramatic and enjoy making your presence felt. You are optimistic, positive, and have high hopes for the future. You are generous, warm, loving, and forgiving. You are frequently impulsive. You have all the drive and charisma necessary to become a successful leader.

Orange

If orange is your favorite color you are able to get along with everyone. You are warm and friendly. You are well organized and efficient. You can organize others as well as yourself. You enjoy activity and are good at motivating yourself. Unless all this activity is directed toward a goal of some sort, you will feel restless and impatient.

Yellow

If yellow is your favorite color you know how to express yourself well, and you thrive on new and different experiences. You enjoy entertaining and being entertained. You communicate well with others, and are full of good ideas. You have an excellent sense of humor, and can be the life and soul of a party when you want to be.

Green

If green is your favorite color you are even-tempered, compassionate, tolerant, supportive, and easy to get along with. You enjoy helping others and may seek a career in a field that enables you to do this full-time. You are both a humanitarian and a natural healer. You have a good mind and enjoy taking care of details. You are stubborn when necessary, but prefer to avoid arguments.

Blue

While the most popular color choice for extroverts is red, introverts usually choose blue. However, just as some introverts choose red because it gives them confidence, so will some extroverts choose blue because it gives them the peace and tranquillity that they lack. If blue is your favorite color you have a creative mind and a good imagination. You are shrewd and perceptive, and enjoy coming up with money-making ideas. There is a quiet, deep side to you also, and you need time for introspection. You hate being hemmed in or restricted in any way, and are happiest when you have something exciting to look forward to. You are adventurous, and this may get you into trouble at times. However, luck always seems to be on your side.

Indigo

If indigo is your favorite color you are reserved, sensitive, emotional, and intuitive. You are gentle, supportive, and caring. You tend to fall in love easily, and are sometimes hurt by the comments and attitudes of others. The central focus of your life is likely to be family and friends. You are responsible and enjoy solving problems.

Violet

If violet is your favorite color you are sophisticated, analytical, discriminating, spiritual and highly intuitive. Because you are introspective and reserved, you need plenty of time on your own. You enjoy study and like to delve deep to find hidden truths. You have your own unique point of view and prefer to do things in your own way.

Silver

If silver is your favorite color you are honest, chivalrous, and idealistic. You have good self-esteem and enjoy helping others. Your friends and colleagues have earned their respect from you, and you feel disillusioned whenever this trust and respect is broken. You are modest about your own accomplishments, and seldom seek fame or recognition for yourself. You are highly intuitive.

Gold

If gold is your favorite color you are ambitious and desire the very best that life can offer. You are extremely capable and charismatic. Your drive, energy, inner strength, and practicality make it almost inevitable that you will rise to the top of your field. Your creative mind provides you with unorthodox solutions to problems.

Brown

If brown is your favorite color you are down-to-earth, practical, and hard working. You are honest, stable, supportive and secure. You view situations in terms of black and white, and have the ability to see the essence of a problem at a glance. This enables you to quickly resolve problems that other people have given up on. It also enables you to buy good quality items, rather than something that just happens to be in fashion. You seldom seek the spotlight, and keep most of your thoughts to yourself.

Black

If black is your favorite color you are an independent thinker with strong opinions on most subjects. You speak your mind. You are disciplined, secretive, and intense. You are goal-oriented and have strong ambitions that other people may not realize you have until they have been achieved.

If you have chosen black because you are feeling depressed, call on a friend for help and company. Make some plans and do something different to cheer yourself up.

White

If white is your favorite color you are gentle, quiet, and nurturing. You thrive on encouragement. You like time on your own and may need to push yourself to spend more time with others. You dislike noisy parties, preferring to spend your time with a few close friends.

White is an unusual choice for a favorite color, and generally indicates that you are in a transition period of your life.

Colors You Dislike

As you can see, your favorite color reveals a great deal about you. Most people have a favorite color, but not many have colors that they dislike. However, it can be useful to have a color of this sort. This is because the color that you hate the most helps you locate your areas of weakness.

Red

If you dislike red you will need to learn how to control and handle your emotional outbursts. These help you eliminate your feelings of anger, but are likely to disturb and upset others.

Orange

If you dislike orange you will have deep-rooted feelings of insecurity and feel frustrated and thwarted whenever anything goes wrong.

Yellow

If you dislike yellow you will be easily intimidated by others. You will have a fear of criticism and hold yourself back, rather than attempt something and face the risk of being criticized.

Green

If you dislike green you are likely to suffer from procrastination and lack of motivation. You are likely to get bored easily.

Blue

If you dislike blue you are likely to feel constantly stressed and could suffer from psychosomatic illnesses.

Indigo

If you dislike indigo you are likely to feel rejected or unvalued by others.

Violet

If you dislike violet you are likely to feel intimidated by the beliefs and rules of others. You are likely to feel that other people undervalue or ignore your faith and spirituality.

Silver

If you dislike silver you are likely to feel let down by the actions of others. You could feel disillusioned, disappointed, and hurt.

Gold

If you dislike gold you are likely to have decided that your dreams of success will never be realized, and that you are doomed to failure and mediocrity.

Brown

If you dislike brown you are likely to be fearful, timid, and withdrawn. You will probably worry incessantly about everything that is going on in your life.

Black

If you dislike black you probably underrate your own abilities. You will fail to recognize your good qualities, focusing instead on your perceived failings.

White

If you dislike white you will feel like an outsider, never feeling completely comfortable in any situation. You are likely to be lonely and find it hard to make friends.

You probably found the colors you liked and disliked revealed more about you than you expected. Adding another color to this exercise makes it even more revealing. In the next chapter we'll look at the colors that support you.

CHAPTER SEVEN

COLORS OF SUPPORT

Colors are amazingly supportive. More than twenty years ago, I knew a woman who had been promoted to a senior management role in a company that had previously had only male managers. As her division was doing better than the others, she was asked to give a talk to all the other senior managers to tell them what she was doing that was working so well. My friend was extremely capable and confident in most situations. However, she was terrified at the thought of giving a talk to all her male colleagues, as she thought they were unhappy with her promotion and rapid rise up the company ladder.

I suggested that she wear a little bit of red to give her additional confidence. In fact, she did much more than that. She dressed entirely in red and gave a dynamic address that her colleagues remembered for years afterwards. This is a good example of how color can alter your attitude. While she was dressed in red my friend had more than enough confidence to give an inspiring speech. It is unlikely she could have given the same speech if she had worn a black suit.

Color can also affect your mood. If you are angry about something your blood pressure is likely to rise. You can calm yourself down by wearing green, or by going for a walk in a park with green grass and green trees. If you feel lacking in energy, try wearing orange. You do not need a large amount. A scarf, tie, or belt of the color you need is all that is required. You will receive better results if the color is visible, but undergarments of the correct color will also help. This is because the body absorbs the vibrations of the colors.

Here are the main colors, along with the feelings that they can change. As you read through these you may realize why you choose to wear certain colors. It can also be a useful exercise to deliberately wear colors that you would not normally choose in order to experience the effects they have on you.

Red

Red is useful for eliminating negative thoughts and to counteract a lack of energy. It overcomes fatigue. You should wear red whenever you are suffering from frustration, apathy, or feelings of hopelessness. It is stimulating, and provides confidence, strength, stamina, enthusiasm, and persistence. It breaks down inhibitions. It can also restore joy and happiness. Wear red on any occasion when it is important that you succeed. Someone once told me that red is a popular color for clothing during wartime as it gives courage.

Red is also a good color to wear after an illness as it generates energy and vitality.

Orange

Orange is useful whenever you feel indecisive or lacking in motivation. It provides confidence and a sense of security. It increases vitality and eliminates procrastination, while helping you focus on what you want to achieve. It also enhances all close relationships, and makes you more sociable and outgoing. You should wear orange if you are fearful, anxious, or find it hard to spend much time on your own. It is particularly useful if you have had a shock or heard some bad news.

Yellow

Yellow helps you overcome frustration, loneliness, and depression. It is mentally stimulating and promotes concentration, good ideas, and clear thinking. It encourages you to communicate with others, and helps stimulate feelings of joy, happiness, and excitement. You should wear yellow if you have a tendency to take things too seriously, or underestimate yourself. It is particularly useful if you are feeling depressed. Yellow clothing makes you feel good about yourself.

Green

Green is a restful color that eliminates tension, anger, impatience, and emotional problems. It creates stability, clear thinking, and the ability to understand the views of others. It is calming, healing, restful, and supportive. You should wear green whenever you feel hemmed in, restricted, have a sense of loss, or are suffering from emotional stress.

Blue

Blue is the color of integrity and calmness. It eliminates fears, anxiety, and nervousness. It creates confidence, leadership capabilities, and the ability to look ahead calmly and dispassionately. You should wear blue whenever you are stressed or feel you might overreact to a situation or circumstance. Blue is also a useful color to wear if you have to spend time with people who drain your energy. I call these people "psychic vampires."

Indigo

Indigo reduces the effects of phobias and emotional stress. It eliminates negativity. It allows you to make contact with your intuition and to trust others again. It enhances your spirituality and enables you to find peace, fulfillment, and joy inside yourself. It is also mentally stimulating and is a good color to wear when you are studying. You should wear indigo whenever you feel uncertain about a new situation or need to make future plans. It is also a useful color to wear if you suffer from headaches.

Violet

Violet reduces guilt, worry, stress, and feelings of inadequacy. It allows you to find inner peace and a sense of security. It promotes feelings of universal love that enable you to look at other people without judging or criticizing them. Violet also encourages creativity. You should wear violet or purple whenever you feel nervous or need protection from the demands of others. You should also wear violet when you find yourself in a situation where you may drink or eat too much.

Silver

Silver is useful when you feel inadequate or unsure of your self-worth. It helps you gain enough confidence to start trusting others again.

Gold

Gold helps eliminate self-sabotaging feelings about money and success. It provides confidence and the self-discipline to keep on persevering until you reach your goal. It also helps you seek wisdom, knowledge, and truth. You should wear gold whenever you cease trusting in your intuition.

Brown

Brown helps eliminate panic attacks, anxiety, and emotional insecurity. It grounds you to the earth and helps you keep matters in proportion. Brown is one of the main colors of nature. It is warming and life-affirming. You should wear brown whenever you feel frightened or uncertain about the future, or need to feel safe and secure.

White

White helps eliminate the negative feelings of being overwhelmed by the needs of others. It provides spiritual protection and a sense of peace amidst hectic activity. You should wear white whenever you feel worried or anxious, or need to express yourself clearly. It is also a useful color to wear when you are looking for a major change, or have started following a new direction. You will find colds disappear more quickly when you wear white. Pale-colored clothing encourages light to pass into and out of the body, enhancing your mood and encouraging healing.

Black

Black provides strength and the ability to stand up for yourself when other people are trying to take advantage. It helps eliminate oversensitivity and heightened emotions. However, it also acts as an emotional barrier that keeps people at a distance.

Obviously, most of the time you will wear combinations of colors. You might, for instance, wear a blue business suit because you feel comfortable wearing that color. However, if you add a red scarf or handkerchief you will subliminally send out the message that you can be assertive when necessary.

When buying clothes you should think about the colors that are best suited to you. However, you should also consider the colors that make you feel safe and secure, and the reasons why you are buying these particular clothes. The clothes you wear to a job interview may not be the same ones you wear to a casual lunch with friends.

You will find wearing supportive colors extremely beneficial. In addition to wearing them, you can also introduce these colors into your home and workspace in other ways to provide you with support whenever necessary.

You also have other colors of support. These are derived from your astrology sign and will be covered in more detail in chapter 10.

Using specific colors to look after your aura is another form of support and protection. Meditation is one of the most effective ways of doing this. Meditating on different colors to protect your aura is the subject of the next chapter.

CHAPTER EIGHT

MEDITATING WITH COLOR

There are many myths about meditation. Some people consider it to be a form of escapism, while others feel it is the perfect way to make contact with your inner being. Meditation is state of relaxed contemplation. It allows you to physically relax and gain access to the insights of your subconscious mind. At its best, it will give you access to the divine forces and allow you to clearly understand your purpose in this incarnation. Meditation allows you to view life in a completely different way and enhances your physical, mental, emotional, and spiritual bodies.

Mini-Meditation

You perform a mini-meditation whenever you pause for a few moments to reflect on something. You probably do this many times every day. You might see a bird fly overhead, or a magnificent sunset, and think about the wonders of nature for a second or two. You might take a sip of coffee and reflect for a moment on the smell, taste, and feelings of pleasure that drinking coffee provides. Meditations do not need to be profound or spiritual. All meditation is of value. Mini-meditations like these help you appreciate the pleasures and delights of life, while also filling you with a sense of purpose, compassion, and understanding. If people call you a dreamer, take it as a compliment. I certainly do. You do not need to sit in the lotus position to meditate. You can take a mini-meditation while going for a walk, doing the dishes, shopping, or doing almost any other activity. It is a perfectly normal and natural activity.

You can also create a mini-meditation whenever you wish. If you need more energy, for instance, close your eyes for a few seconds and picture yourself completely surrounded by a magnificent red. If you're concentrating on a problem, close your eyes and visualize yellow. I like to surround myself with whichever color I need. You may prefer to mentally picture an object of the color you need. Maybe you'll see a bright green door or an ornament of the color you need.

Meditation 101

Mini-meditations occur spontaneously. For a more formal, organized meditation you will need a quiet place where you will not be disturbed or bothered. Wear loose-fitting, comfortable clothes. Many people like to meditate while sitting in a straight-backed chair with the backs of their hands resting on their thighs or lap. However, if you find it hard to relax in that position, it is perfectly acceptable to sit in a more comfortable chair or lie down on a bed or the floor. I'm inclined to fall asleep when meditating in a bed, but I sometimes meditate on a recliner chair. Most of the time I prefer a straight-backed chair. You want to be comfortable, but not too comfortable.

Make sure the room is warm enough, as you are likely to lose a degree or two of body heat during the course of the meditation. You might like to cover yourself with a blanket. This provides subliminal feelings of security and safety, and may make it easier for you to relax, while at the same time keeping you warm.

If you are sitting in a chair you may want to roll your shoulders and shake your arms before starting. You want to be as relaxed as possible.

When you are ready, close your eyes and take a few slow, deep breaths until your breathing slows down. The first stage of the meditation is to temporarily release all your everyday worries and concerns. I find it helpful to imagine a beautiful, secret room. Whenever I go into this room I automatically release all tensions and concerns, as every aspect of my life is perfect whenever I am inside it. My room is an imaginary place. You might like to create an imaginary scene for yourself, or perhaps go to a place you have been in the past where you felt totally relaxed, serene, and happy. Your imaginary scene might be completely different than mine. You might choose a magnificent bathroom and relax in a warm bubble bath. One of my students told me about that particular visualization. A log cabin, out in the woods, might make a good choice. You might choose to visit a favorite place from your childhood. If you loved visiting your grandparents, for instance, you might choose to visit them again in your imagination.

If you choose to create an imaginary place, you can place anything you wish inside it. My secret room has lush carpet, comfortable furniture, and beautiful paintings on the walls. It is always pleasantly warm. I can see the room clearly in my mind, and my body immediately relaxes whenever I picture it. Consequently, this is the place I go to first, whenever I meditate.

It might take time and practice before you can go to your secret place and immediately relax. You may have a particular worry or concern that you find hard to discard even inside your secret place. If this occurs, focus on the concern. Think about whatever it happens to be for as long as you wish. Once you have done this, give the concern a color and a shape. In your mind's eye, allow the shape to grow larger and smaller. Notice how your concerns grow as the shape increases in size, but also discover that your concerns diminish as the shape gets smaller. Make the shape as small as you can, and then release it from your secret place. You might decide to attach it to a helium balloon so that it floats away. You may place it in a sink and then turn the tap on so that it disappears down the drain. You might open the door of your secret room and place the shape on the doormat. Again, it makes no difference what you do, just as long as you place your concerns outside your secret place for the duration of your meditation.

Now that your worries and concerns have been temporarily put aside, you can start focusing on your breathing. Take steady, rhythmic breaths. As you inhale, say to yourself: "relaxation coming in." As you exhale, say silently: "tension and stress going out."

Continue doing this for as long as you can. You will find yourself distracted with other thoughts that come into your mind. Dismiss them as you become aware of them, and focus on your breathing and the two phrases you are saying to yourself.

It is a good idea to stop at this point if you have not meditated before. Open your eyes, and sit or lie down quietly for a minute or two before carrying on with your day. Repeat the meditation up to this stage several times over the next week or two and see if you can extend the length of time you spend focusing on your breathing without extraneous thoughts breaking in. You will find the regular practice highly beneficial, and it will become easier and easier to leave your cares and worries outside your secret place.

Now it is time to move a step further and find the stillness within. In your mind's eye focus on a spot just above your navel. Inhale deeply and exhale slowly. As you exhale, silently say the word "ten." Continue to focus on the spot just above your navel as you take nine more deep breaths and count down to one.

Forget about your breathing and allow yourself to sink deeply into the area above your navel. Enjoy the pleasant, comfortable, tranquil sensation for as long as you wish. When you have had enough, allow your concentration to return to your head, and focus on your breathing again.

Picture yourself in your secret place, and then, mentally, return to the present. Visualize your surroundings for a few moments before opening your eyes. When you feel ready, stand up and stretch.

You are likely to feel excited and full of energy after your first meditation. However, some people feel slightly tired and stiff. Everyone is different.

You may feel that you reached inside yourself and made contact with your soul, your subconscious mind, or at least the stillness within. Conversely, you may feel slightly disappointed because you relaxed but didn't go anywhere.

It is natural to feel disappointed, but all it means is that you need to practice. Reaching the stillness within is something everyone can do. Some find it easily, while others have to work at it.

It is highly likely that you almost reached the stillness within. You may have a sense of frustration that you almost got there, but couldn't quite reach it. You may even have reached it for a split second, but were unable to stay there. If this is the case, congratulate yourself on what you did achieve, and experiment again later.

There are two main reasons why people fail to achieve the desired state. By far the most common reason is that people rush through the breathing and relaxation stages because they want to reach their desired goal. If you feel you may have done this, take each step more slowly next time. Enjoy the process, and spend plenty of time in your secret place before moving on.

The other possibility is that you were overanxious about the whole process. If this applies to you, experiment again, but with an attitude that you don't care if you are successful or not. You are simply going to enjoy the experiment.

Practice your meditation on a regular basis. Twice a day would be ideal. Most people tell me their days are too busy to do this. However, it is when you are busiest that you need to slow down. A brief mini-meditation in the middle of the day will make you more productive in the afternoon than you would be without it.

The key to successful meditation is breathing and re-laxation. The benefits of meditation are so enormous that it is worth any amount of time invested in learning how to do it.

The Power of Words

Once you are able to reach the inner stillness within, you will be able to use this ability in many different ways. A useful exercise is to think about different words while in this state. Incidentally, this is also a good experiment to demonstrate the power of meditation.

Choose a word that is meaningful to you. Peace, life, love, kindness, hope, honesty, truth, and destiny are all good examples of words you might use. Sit down for a few moments and write down everything that the word suggests to you.

The next step is to meditate on the word. Relax and go into meditation. Once you reach this state, say the word you have chosen silently to yourself. You may prefer to say it out loud. Pause and see what impressions and ideas come to you. You may find yourself overwhelmed with images, pictures, and ideas. If this occurs, observe them all so that you can recall them when you return from your meditation.

If nothing much occurs to you, you will have to adopt a different approach. Think of the word and turn it into a shape and color. Allow the shape to grow small and then large in your mind. Turn it into a ball and bounce it, and then toss it into the air and catch it again. Have fun with the shape, all the while remaining aware that it is your chosen word. After doing this for a minute or two, hold the shape in the palms of your hands and give it a mouth, eyes, ears and nose. Ask the shape to tell you something about itself. Again see what comes to you.

The next step is to hold this word while walking through a rainbow. Slowly walk into the red and allow the rays of red to penetrate to every cell of your body. Ask the word how it responds to the color red. When you feel ready, move into the orange and allow your body to feel rejuvenated with the orange ray. Again, ask the word how it feels about the color orange. Repeat with every color of the rainbow, until you emerge from the violet into the clear fresh air.

You must release the word before coming out of the meditation. You might want to hold it in your cupped hands and gently blow it away. You might attach it to a balloon and let it float up and out of sight. You might place it on a shelf and watch it dissolve away to nothing. It doesn't matter how you let it go, as long as it is set free.

Once you have done that, take a few deep breaths, move your body slightly, stretch, and then open your eyes. Write down any insights that have occurred to you about the word before carrying on with your day. It is important that you do this before moving on to other activities. The information you have obtained is like a dream and is quickly forgotten. You must record it as soon as possible.

Healing the World Meditation

This meditation uses three colors: pink, yellow, and blue. Relax in the normal way and enter into a meditative state. Visualize yourself surrounded by a pure white light of protection. Allow this white to slowly change to a beautiful rose pink. Feel and sense the delicate healing energies of this magnificent color. Each time you inhale you are absorbing rose pink energy that is sent to every cell of your body. When you feel yourself filled to overflowing with this color, send it out into the universe to comfort and heal others. Visualize it spreading out from you in waves of rose pink energy that ultimately encircle the entire world.

Picture the rose pink energy for as long as you can, and then allow it to gradually change into a pure yellow. Feel the warmth, energy, and vitality of the yellow. Allow it to penetrate and revitalize every cell of your body. Visualize it as a circle of energy inside your solar plexus. Feel a sense of love for the world and everything within it, and then send that love out to everyone who needs it as waves of perfect yellow energy.

Once you have done this, allow the yellow to gradually transform into blue until you are completely surrounded by swirling mists of the most gorgeous blue you can imagine. Feel it purifying and healing you with every breath you take. Again, when you feel ready, send this perfect blue energy out into the world for everyone who needs it.

Finally, allow the blue to slowly transform into the pure white light again, and feel comfortable and at peace inside it. Give thanks to the universal spirit for all the blessings in your life, and for enabling you to spread healing energy to people who need it.

When you feel ready, take a few deep breaths, stretch, and open your eyes.

Forgiving Others Meditation

This is another meditation that you'll find revealing and revitalizing. It is intended to help you release any negativity that prevents you from enjoying a deep sense of peace, happiness, and contentment. Although this meditation is intended to help you forgive others for anything they have done to you, and to forgive yourself for any harm you may have done to others, it can also be used to let go of any form of anger, sorrow, pain, and hurt.

Relax and enter the meditative state. Once you have reached this place, imagine yourself surrounded, cushioned, and protected by a healing white light. Think about someone who has hurt you in the past. Visualize this person inside the healing white light, and send that person a color, along with your love and forgiveness. You will not need to choose this color, as the right one will come into your mind as you send your message to the other person. Sense that person absorbing the color and your message, and then fading from view. You have forgiven that person unconditionally, and there is no need to think of him or her again.

Repeat this with all the people who have hurt you in the past. Forgive each and every one of them. Make sure you have included every person you can possibly think of who has had a negative effect upon your life. Some of these people might be strangers. If someone cut you off on the road a week ago, send that anonymous person love, healing and forgiveness.

Once you have done that, send yourself love and healing. Forgive yourself for everything that you have done, deliberately or accidentally. Enjoy the feeling of release as you let go of all the negativity inside yourself. Now is the time to let go of any grievances or anything else that prevents you from achieving inner peace.

The final step is to expand the white light that surrounds you until it completely encircles the world. See yourself as a vital, essential part of the universal life force. Now that you have let go of all the negativity you can use your energy to improve our planet for the benefit of everyone.

Enjoy this state for as long as possible. When you feel ready, take three deep breaths, stretch, and open your eyes.

Compassionate Meditation

Compassionate meditation is similar to the last two, because it is designed to send thoughts of love and compassion to all humanity. An article in the *Proceedings of the National Academy of Sciences of the United States of America* (Nov. 8, 2004) reported on an experiment conducted on eight Buddhist monks. The researchers found that gamma wave activity in the monks' brains increased markedly when they were performing a compassionate meditation. In fact, the level of gamma wave activity was the highest the researchers had ever recorded. Gamma wave activity is involved with mental processes, such as learning, concentration, perception, and memory. Areas of the brain that are associated with positive emotions also showed increased activity. This experiment indicates that meditating on a regular basis will make you happier, and better able to understand and learn.[1] It also shows how beneficial it can be to perform a brief meditation before beginning a mentally involved task.

You can perform a compassionate meditation at any time. All you need do is close your eyes, take a few deep breaths, relax, and then generate feelings of love and compassion for all humanity. Allow these feelings to swirl around you like a cloud, and then filter into every cell of your body.

When you feel ready, ask the feelings to give you a color to symbolize love and compassion. Allow your cloud of compassion to be permeated with this color, and then let it grow and expand as you mentally send your feelings out into the world.

Remain in this state for as long as you wish. To return to your everyday life, take a slow deep breath, smile as you exhale, and then open your eyes.

Seven Rays Meditation

This meditation is a form of creative visualization that uses all the colors of the rainbow. It is intended to give you all the benefits of walking through the rainbow, but in a slightly different way.

Relax and enter the meditative state. Visualize yourself in your secret place, and see a beautiful painting of a landscape hanging on a wall. If your secret place is outdoors, the painting might be leaning against a tree or table. The painting is so beautiful that you get closer and closer to it, until you are suddenly inside it. Now you are walking through lush green grass and gazing at the beautiful trees as you walk through the countryside. You are enjoying the walk, and the slight breeze makes the leaves of the trees murmur as you walk under them. You walk up a rise and sit down at the summit, looking around at the countryside that spreads out in all directions. In the distance you can see the sea. It's a deep indigo color, and you can see a few white flecks on the waves.

You lie down on the grass and gaze up at the clear blue sky. A few fluffy clouds appear to frolic in the sunlight, but your overall sensation is of the wonderful, beautiful, clear blue of the sky. After a while you decide to start walking again. You get up and look around you. To your left is a large floral garden that you decide to explore. Someone has planted daffodils in the grass and you pause to admire them. They are the most beautiful yellow that you have ever seen.

You continue on to the formal garden and see that the border of the garden is full of sunflowers. You gaze at their orange centers and think of the healing rays of the sun. Inside the garden, most of the flowers are roses. You particularly enjoy the differing shades of the red roses. You marvel at their perfection.

You see now that this garden is planted in front of a large building with several marble pillars in the front. You walk up the marble steps to the main entrance. It is obviously a temple of some sort. There is a soft glow coming from the entrance. You see why when you walk inside. The entire lobby area is a magnificent violet color, and you feel a sense of peace and tranquillity. You are alone, but you suddenly feel the presence of the divine.

You look outside, but decide to carry on exploring the interior of the building. Ahead of you are seven doors, each painted a different color of the rainbow. You open the red door and discover that the room behind it is completely red. There is red carpet, wallpaper, furniture, and lighting. Each of the other rooms also reflects the color shown on the door. You spend a bit of time visiting the rooms that appeal to you, and then go outside again. You sit on the top step and gaze around at the glorious landscape.

All too soon, it is time to leave. You walk through the garden again, up to the top of the rise and down the other side to where you started. You see the back of the picture frame and climb through it, returning to your secret place. You look back at the picture; you are sorry that you have had to leave, but you know that you can return any time you wish to be bathed by all the colors of the rainbow.

Take a few slow deep breaths, stretch, and open your eyes.

Chakra Meditation

Meditation provides an effective way of gaining an increased understanding of your chakras. Relax and enter into the meditative state. When you are ready, focus your attention on your root chakra at the base of your spine. Notice how it grounds you to the earth, and provides you with a sense of security. Add red to your mental picture and see if your feelings change in any way. Observe the images and thoughts that come to you as you focus on your root chakra.

You can stop at this point, if you wish. Alternatively, you might want to explore each of the other chakras in turn to see what insights come to you.

Focusing on your sacral chakra may give you insights into your sexuality, emotions, and how you experience pleasure. Your solar plexus chakra may tell you how much joy there is in your life. Your heart chakra might give you insight into love and relationships. Your throat chakra might offer suggestions on how you communicate with others and help you become more creative. Your brow chakra may provide ideas to develop your imagination, vision, and clairvoyance. Finally, your crown chakra might help you understand, know, and gain a closer connection with the universe.

Another fascinating and enjoyable way to meditate with color is to draw a mandala. That is the subject of the next chapter.

CHAPTER NINE

MANDALAS

Mandalas are designs that were originally drawn to symbolize the universe. They are described as sacred art because they symbolize spiritual, cosmic, and psychic order. They are used both for meditation and for sacred rites. Mandalas can be made in any shape, but are usually circular. This is not surprising, since the word *mandala* is a Sanskrit word that means circle. In effect, a magic circle is a form of mandala, as it contains the energy that is created during the ritual, while providing protection at the same time.

Mandalas are useful tools for focusing the mind. In the East they are frequently used in this way to help gain spiritual and clairvoyant insights. The person symbolically enters into the mandala in the course of his or her meditation and becomes spiritually renewed.

You may have seen or heard about the beautiful sand mandalas that Tibetan monks create. They are called *dultson-kyil-khor*, which means "mandala of colored powders." The monks spend days constructing a magnificent, colorful mandala by pouring colored sand through a fine metal funnel. The process begins by consecrating the ground the mandala will be constructed on. The outline of the mandala is then drawn in white ink, and the mandala is constructed from the center outwards. This symbolizes creation from a single cell to an entire world. The traditional colors for Tibetan mandalas are white, red, yellow, green, and blue. Gold is sometimes used, also.

Typically, the mandala consists of an outer square that encloses one, two, three, or four concentric circles. The outermost circle is a symbolic ring of fire. This keeps the uninitiated out and also symbolizes the burning of ignorance. Inside this circle is a ring of diamonds that symbolizes illumination, another ring that symbolizes eight graveyards signifying perception, and an inner circle of lotus leaves that symbolize spiritual rebirth. Inside these circles is another square divided into four triangles by lines joining the opposite corners. Each triangle contains another circle inside it. A fifth circle is drawn in the center of the mandala. Inside these are placed symbols of five divinities.

The process of creating the mandala provides enormous healing energy. Once the mandala is complete, its role is over, and a ceremony is conducted to release the healing energy into the world. The mandala is destroyed by sweeping the sand in to the center of the circle and placing it into an urn. The sand is poured into a nearby river. From here it ultimately reaches the ocean and travels around the world spreading peace and harmony everywhere it reaches.

Mandalas are also used for therapeutic purposes. This is because they clearly reveal the artist's moods and feelings at the time he or she created it.

Artists have always known this, of course, but Carl Jung (1875–1961), the great Swiss psychiatrist, was the first to discover just how beneficial it was for mental and emotional healing. His patients clearly revealed their most intimate feelings and moods inside the mandalas they created. They were able to exorcise themselves, and release their pain and trauma, by constructing mandalas.

Jung felt that mandalas were archetypal symbols of mankind's quest for psychic integration. Although he painted his first mandala in 1916, he did not fully understand them for another two or three years, and it took another ten years for him to introduce them to the psychology profession. In his autobiography, *Memories, Dreams, Reflections*, Jung wrote: "I sketched every morning in a notebook a small circular drawing, a mandala, which seemed to correspond to my inner situation at the time. With the help of these drawings I could observe my psychic transformations from day to day."[1]

Mandalas work so well because images come directly from the soul. Once they are expressed, they lose their effectiveness and can be released, allowing you to move forward again. Words are logical, but get in the way of feelings. Creating a mandala enables you to bypass your logical left brain and deal directly with your soul.

You will experience many benefits once you start drawing mandalas:

1. The process of drawing a mandala is fun. It is creative, and takes you away from your everyday concerns while you are working on it.

2. You will find the process revealing and illuminating. It enables you to make contact with the real you inside and discover the ever-changing pattern of your life on a regular basis.

3. Mandalas help you to contact your higher self, the God within. This opens the door to clairvoyance, precognition, and enlightenment.

4. The process of drawing a mandala is healing and therapeutic. It enables you to release any pain, trauma, or psychic blockages that are holding you back.

Mandalas are usually drawn inside a circle. This is because the circle is the traditional symbol of wholeness, completeness, perfection, unity, and eternity. Consequently, I suggest that you gain experience with circular mandalas before experimenting with other shapes.

All you need are colored pencils, markers, or crayons, white paper, and a well-lit place where you will not be interrupted for at least thirty minutes. Play music and burn candles and incense, if you wish. I prefer silence, but in my experience, most people enjoy having gentle music playing in the background.

Start by drawing a circle on the piece of paper. I usually use a plate as a template. Pause for a few moments before starting. I generally take a few deep breaths and focus on relaxing my body before starting to draw a mandala.

Daily Ritual

Drawing a mandala every day is a useful way to gain experience of the subject. Over a period of time the mandalas you draw will provide a fascinating record of what was going on in your life at the time you drew them. Carl Jung drew a mandala every day.

Spend a few moments in a state of casual, calm awareness before picking up a pencil and starting to draw. It is important that you do not focus much attention on what you are doing. Draw spontaneously. Observe what your hand is doing with mild interest, but draw as little as possible with intent. Allow your hand to draw anything it wants, in the manner it wants to. Your hand will also know when to put one pencil down and pick up another. Your hand will also decide when you are finished.

You may want to examine your mandala right away to see what insights it provides. I usually put mine aside for at least a few hours, as I find them easier to understand when there is a period of time between the drawing and interpretation. Sometimes the meaning of the mandala will be obvious. If you are feeling depressed, for instance, your mandala is likely to contain darker colors and have jagged-looking edges to the designs. If you are feeling happy you will probably use lighter colors and your creation will seem joyful and high-spirited.

Special Purposes

You can also construct mandalas for special purposes. If you are faced with a particular problem, you can think about your concern while constructing a mandala. The finished mandala will provide valuable insights into the matter and will frequently liberate you from the concern. This is because you release the problem into the mandala, and this allows healing, or release, to occur. Frequently, there will be no need to examine the mandala later as you will have moved on and left the problem behind.

When constructing a mandala to resolve a problem, you are permitted to determine the design and colors of the mandala ahead of time. By doing this you can use specific symbols or ideas that you feel will be helpful.

In fact, this can be taken even further. You might want to deliberately construct a simple mandala that you can redraw on a regular basis. Instead of doodling while waiting for someone on the phone, for instance, you can quickly draw your special mandala. Obviously, you may not always be able to draw these doodle-type mandalas in color. This does not matter, as long as the original mandala was done in color. You can visualize the colors in position as you quickly sketch the mandala. In the past, I used to indicate the colors with a letter and an arrow. I would use "Y" for yellow, "B" for blue, etc. I still occasionally do this, but most of the time I simply imagine the colors in their correct positions.

You can create mandalas for any problem. If you need more confidence, for instance, create a mandala that symbolizes courage, strength, self-esteem, and confidence. Draw this mandala as often as possible. Each time you create it, you are absorbing the qualities you desire.

You might create mandalas for vibrant health, financial success, quality relationships, spiritual growth, and for any other area of your life that you wish to develop.

Mandalas of this sort should always be created inside a circle, as this shape provides wholeness and unity.

Questioning Your Mandalas

An interesting way to gain further insights from your mandalas is to have a conversation with them. The replies will come directly from your soul. All you need do is ask a question and wait for a reply. Sometimes I write a question down. At other times I think about it, or say it out loud. After asking the question, I sit in a relaxed state with my eyes closed until the answer comes to me. The response generally comes as a thought that appears in my mind.

However, I have had occasions when a small voice spoke the answer. It is important that you accept the first answer that comes to you. This is the voice of your soul. It is highly likely that you will not receive the response that you expect or desire. This is why many people wait for more insights. Unfortunately, it is the first response that is important. Later responses are more likely to come from your logical left brain and will reflect what is going on in your mind rather than your soul.

If you receive no response from your question, ask another. Keep on doing this until you establish communication. Once you have received a response to your first question you can ask as many additional questions as you wish.

Sometimes the responses you receive will appear to have nothing to do with your question. Ask a few more questions and see if they provide the insights you want. If not, wait a day or two and then ask the questions again.

Chakra Mandalas

After you have experimented with mandalas for a while, you might like to create a series of mandalas that symbolize your chakras. Focus on the specific chakra as you draw it, and visualize the chakra in a state of perfect balance and excellent health.

Obviously, the main color of these chakra mandalas will be determined by the specific chakra. However, you should feel free to utilize as many other colors as you wish.

Once you have created a set of chakra mandalas you can use them in a variety of ways.

1. You can balance all of your chakras by lying down and placing each of the mandalas in position on your body. Relax and visualize each chakra in turn, as it is stimulated and revitalized by the mandalas.

2. You can use a specific mandala to balance any chakra that is underactive. Lie down with the mandala in position for at least five minutes and absorb its energy.

3. If a chakra is overactive, you can create a special mandala to bring it into line. Usually, using the color that is complementary to the color of the chakra does this. (The complementary colors are those that are opposite each other on a color wheel. Red is complementary to green, blue is complementary to orange, and yellow is complementary to violet. Red is also considered complementary to indigo.)

4. If at all possible, place the seven mandalas in a vertical row in a place that you pass frequently. Each time you walk past, the mandalas will strengthen and stimulate your chakras.

Symbol Mandalas

So far, we have been discussing free-form mandalas. Inside the basic shape of the mandala, you have been able to draw anything you wish. Other forms of mandalas are created using geometric symbols, such as squares, circles, triangles, and stars. Indian yantras, which are used for meditation purposes, are constructed solely of geometric shapes.

The central point of these mandalas is the *bindu*, or the central point. The mandala is constructed around this. The center can be looked at as a tiny seed, full of potential. It is a sacred space that contains everything.

You will need compasses and rulers to create a geometric mandala. Once you have finished drawing it, you can then color it in, in any way you desire. The completed mandala is interpreted in the usual way. However, if you wish, you can also interpret the individual geometric shapes. A square, for instance, can be interpreted as security, balance, stability, or even the earth. A triangle sitting on its base is considered a masculine symbol. It also represents the Fire element. A reversed triangle symbolizes the female principle and the moon. A cross is the emblem of the Christian faith, but it also marks the four cardinal directions. A pentagram symbolizes harmony, health, and mankind. You can add an extra dimension to your interpretations of mandalas by including symbolism of this sort. You can also ask yourself why you painted a certain geometrical design a certain color, rather than another. Additional insights can come from this, also.

Other Aspects of the Mandala

Circular mandalas can be considered as a clock face, with 12 o'clock in the north position, 6 o'clock in the south, and 3 and 9 o'clock in the east and west positions. Consequently, you may be able to gain insight into when matters will occur that relate to your mandala.

Generally speaking, everything in the top half of the mandala relates to your conscious mind, while the bottom half symbolizes the subconscious.

Larger Mandalas

Some years ago, I walked along a deserted beach. It was a day or two after a storm and the high-water mark was littered with driftwood and other debris. I didn't make a conscious decision to create a mandala from this material, but suddenly found myself in the middle of a large circle I had created. I found materials of different colors and created a design inside the circle. Finally, I sat down in the middle of this mandala to rest and meditate. I'm not sure how long I sat there, but I felt an enormous sense of happiness and peace when I got up again. Since that time, I've created several large mandalas this way. I particularly enjoy creating them from rocks and stones, but use any material that happens to be available.

All mandalas are valid. There is no such thing as a right or wrong mandala. Every mandala you create is the perfect picture of your subconscious mind at that particular moment. Consequently, there is no need to agonize over your mandalas, and consider them good or bad. There are no prizes for artistic ability or neatness. Neither do you have to show them to anyone else. Have fun with them. Learn from them, and allow them to reveal to you what is important in your own life.

CHAPTER TEN

COLOR SYMBOLISM

Throughout the history of mankind, colors have been laden with symbolism. In every part of the world they have been used to express moods, traits, rank, and position. You have inherited all of this in your genetic makeup. You can perform a simple test to demonstrate this. If someone asked you to associate a color with feeling, thinking, intuition, or sensation, you are likely to name the same colors as almost everyone else, despite being brought up in different cultures.

Folklore is full of color symbolism. Not surprisingly, black is generally considered to be the color of death and mourning, while red is universally a symbol of blood, fire, passion, and life. Green symbolizes nature, rebirth, and hope, while blue depicts the sky and infinity.

Color symbolism has always played an important role in Jewish and Christian mysticism. The Gnostics, for instance, symbolized God the Father as blue, God the Son as yellow, and God the Holy Ghost as red. In Judaism, the divine colors are red, blue, purple, and white. Josephus wrote: "The veils, too, which were composed of four things, they declared the four elements; for the plain [white] linen was proper to signify the earth, because the flax grows out of the earth; the purple signified the sea, because the color is dyed by the blood of a sea shellfish; the blue is fit to signify the air; and the scarlet will naturally be an indication of fire."[1]

This religious interest in color symbolism naturally made its way into Christian art.

Religious Art

Christianity made good use of color, particularly in religious art. Certain colors became associated with particular people or subjects, and could not be used elsewhere. Stained glass was a prime example of this, but it is also easy to detect in most religious art. Here are the main associations:

White

White is the emblem of purity, innocence, virginity, integrity, humility, and life. In religious art, God the Father wore white robes, as did Jesus after his resurrection. The Virgin Mary wears white in pictures of the Assumption (when she was transported to heaven). Psalm 51:7 has the following line: "Wash me, and I shall be whiter than snow."

Red

Red symbolizes divine energy, love, and the Holy Spirit. When used negatively, red also signifies blood, enmity, and punishment. White and red roses in religious art are a sign of innocence and spiritual love.

Yellow

Yellow (and gold) symbolizes the sun, fruitfulness, and the goodness and perfection of God. Joseph, husband of the Virgin Mary, wears yellow. However, yellow also symbolizes the negative qualities of jealousy, deceit, and disloyalty. Not surprisingly, Judas Iscariot is usually shown wearing yellow. The halos of saints are yellow or gold to show the beauty and promise of eternal life.

Green

Green symbolizes spring, hope, and trust in everlasting life. It is also the color of victory. In Buddhist paintings, the Buddha is often shown against a green background. This symbolizes the permanence of life, contrasted with our brief incarnations.

Blue

Blue symbolizes heaven, truth, fidelity, and everlasting life. Jesus and the Virgin Mary usually wear a red tunic and a blue mantle. This signifies love (red) and truth (blue). St. John the Evangelist wears a blue tunic with a red mantle.

Over time, artists gradually changed the color of his tunic to green.

Violet

Violet symbolizes love and spiritual perfection. As it also symbolizes passion and suffering, Christian martyrs frequently wear it. After the crucifixion, the Virgin Mary was depicted wearing violet. Jesus, also, is sometimes shown in violet after his resurrection. As Mary Magdalene is also shown wearing violet robes, this color became associated with everybody who repented their sins.

Gray

Gray symbolizes mourning, sorrow, and humility. Because of this, it was the color first worn by Franciscans, who became known as "the Gray Friars."

Black

Black symbolizes death, mourning, evil, sin, and darkness. Satan, the Prince of Darkness, wears black. Jesus is sometimes shown wearing black in paintings of the Temptation. This symbolizes the entangling, enveloping measures used by Satan. Interestingly, white and black together symbolizes purity. This is why the Carmelites and Dominicans wear these colors.

Astrological Colors

Color has played a role in astrology for thousands of years. The ancient Babylonians and Assyrians built ziggurats, or towers, for astrological purposes. They looked like circular sandcastles, with each level painted a different color. There were usually several levels, symbolizing the seven known planets. When the great temple of Nebuchadnezzar at Barsippa was uncovered, it was found that the seven levels were each decorated in a different color. The bottom level was black to represent Saturn. The second level was orange to represent Jupiter, the third level was red for Mars, the fourth yellow for the sun, the fifth green for Venus, and the sixth blue for Mercury. The top level was dedicated to the Moon and is believed to have been white.

Colors play a role in both the signs and the planets in astrology. You might feel an affinity for one of the colors that relates to your sign. Some color attributions go back many thousands of years. I have placed these early attributions in brackets:

- Aries: (Red)
- Taurus: Yellow, Pink, Pale Blue, (Bright Green)
- Gemini: Violet, Yellow, (Brown)
- Cancer: Green, Gray, (White, Silver)
- Leo: Orange, (Gold)
- Virgo: Violet, Navy Blue, Dark Gray
- Libra: Yellow, Pale Blue, Pink, Green
- Scorpio: Red, (Vermilion)
- Sagittarius: Purple, (Sky Blue)
- Capricorn: Blue, Dark Green, (Black)

• Aquarius: Indigo, (Gray)

• Pisces: Indigo, (Sea Blue)

As you can see, there are a number of possible color choices. Over the years, people have come up with different systems and correspondences, and this sometimes creates confusion. Possibly in an attempt to create a standardized system, the Hermetic Order of the Golden Dawn devised yet another system of color correspondences. They wanted the twelve signs to relate to the seven colors in the rainbow. Here is what they came up with:

• Aries: Red

• Taurus: Red/Orange

• Gemini: Orange

• Cancer: Yellow/Orange

• Leo: Yellow

• Virgo: Yellow/Green

• Libra: Green

• Scorpio: Blue/Green

• Sagittarius: Blue

• Capricorn: Indigo

• Aquarius: Violet

• Pisces: Red/Violet

I prefer the color associations that ancient astrologers devised. However, this is a personal choice, and you should use the system that resonates best for you.

Some people relate the colors of the rainbow to each day of the week, and this then gets related to the planet of the day:

- Sun: Red (Sunday)
- Moon: Orange (Monday)
- Mars: Yellow (Tuesday)
- Mercury: Green (Wednesday)
- Jupiter: Blue (Thursday)
- Venus: Indigo (Friday)
- Saturn: Violet (Saturday)

I find the following list more helpful. I have included the day of the week that each planet represents. This can be useful when you want to use the color for a specific day:

- Sun: Yellow, Gold, Orange (Sunday)
- Moon: Blue, White, Silver, Gray (Monday)
- Mars: Red, Orange, Pink (Tuesday)
- Mercury: Orange, Purple, Silver (Wednesday)
- Jupiter: Violet, Blue (Thursday)
- Venus: Green, Pink, White (Friday)
- Saturn: Indigo, Gray (Saturday)

For thousands of years, certain days have been considered more fortunate that others. The Roman senate did not meet on Fridays, for instance, because it was considered a dangerous day. Here are the fortunate and unfortunate days:

Fortunate Days

- Monday: Moon—peaceful and calm
- Wednesday: Mercury—success
- Thursday: Jupiter—courage, persistence, willpower
- Sunday: Sun—happiness and rest

Unfortunate Days

- Tuesday: Mars—struggles, disagreements, failure
- Friday: Venus—passion
- Saturday: Saturn—danger, catastrophe, death

As well as determining the colors for each day, you can take it several steps further and determine the colors for each hour. These hours are not exactly sixty minutes long as the day is divided into two periods: from sunrise to sunset, and from sunset to sunrise. Each of these periods is divided by twelve to create what are known as "planetary hours." In winter, the daylight planetary hours are considerably less than sixty minutes long, while the nighttime hours are longer. The opposite applies in summer.

The planetary hours start at sunrise and finish at sunrise the next day. Consequently, any hour before sunrise belongs to the previous planetary day.

The order of planets is determined by the day of the week. The planet for the day also represents the first hour of the day, and the other hours follow in sequence. Consequently, the Sun rules the first hour of Sunday, because, as you know, the Sun represents Sunday. Likewise, the Moon represents the first hour of Monday, Mars the first hour of Tuesday, and so on. Here are the twenty-four hours of Sunday:

- Hour One: Sun, Yellow (Sunrise)
- Hour Two: Venus, Green
- Hour Three: Mercury, Red
- Hour Four: Moon, Blue
- Hour Five: Saturn, Indigo
- Hour Six: Jupiter, Violet
- Hour Seven: Mars, Orange
- Hour Eight: Sun, Yellow
- Hour Nine: Venus, Green
- Hour Ten: Mercury, Red
- Hour Eleven: Moon, Blue
- Hour Twelve: Saturn, Indigo
- Hour Thirteen: Jupiter, Violet
- Hour Fourteen: Mars, Orange
- Hour Fifteen: Sun, Yellow
- Hour Sixteen: Venus, Green
- Hour Seventeen: Mercury, Red
- Hour Eighteen: Moon, Blue
- Hour Nineteen: Saturn, Indigo
- Hour Twenty: Jupiter, Violet

- Hour Twenty-one: Mars, Orange
- Hour Twenty-two: Sun, Yellow
- Hour Twenty-three: Venus, Green
- Hour Twenty-four: Mercury, Red

This information can add another dimension to your magic. You might gain additional benefit by performing a particular spell or ritual during the planetary hour that is associated with the color or planet that relates best to your desire. Planetary hours are extremely important when making amulets or talismans.[2] You might also choose a certain hour because that planet rules your astrology sign. Here is a list of these:

- The Sun rules Leo
- The Moon rules Cancer
- Mercury rules Gemini and Virgo
- Mars rules Aries (Scorpio)
- Venus rules Taurus and Libra
- Jupiter rules Sagittarius (Pisces)
- Saturn rules Capricorn (Aquarius)
- Uranus rules Aquarius
- Neptune rules Pisces
- Pluto rules Scorpio

Of course, the ancient astrologers had no knowledge of Uranus, Neptune, and Pluto. Consequently, Aquarius was assigned to Saturn, Pisces to Jupiter, and Scorpio to Mars.

Tarot Cards

The tarot deck consists of seventy-eight cards. The colorful designs and pictures on these are rich in symbolism, and color plays a part in this. Here are the cards that relate specifically to the main colors:

- Red: The Chariot
- Orange: The Empress
- Yellow: The Sun
- Green: Temperance
- Blue: The Magician
- Indigo: The World
- Violet: The Emperor
- Pink: The Lovers
- Magenta: The Hermit
- White: The Star
- Brown: The Devil
- Black: Death
- Gray: Justice

You can use these cards in a number of ways. You may choose to carry a card with you as a protective amulet. Both the card and the color energy you are seeking would determine the specific card you would choose to use. You might place a certain tarot card on your altar when performing a ritual. This card might be used to provide a specific color, but at the same time it would also add the energy of the card.

I enjoy meditating with tarot cards. Sometimes I use a small number of cards from a single deck. At other times, I decide on a card and take that card from several different decks. This allows me to study the choices that different artists have made to illustrate the card. It is fascinating to ponder why they made certain color choices.

Flower Magic

A number of books have been published that give the meanings of individual flowers. A rose indicates love, for instance. (I once heard a comedian say that a single rose says much more than that. It also says: "I'm cheap!") Fortunately, we can do much more with flowers than that. Here is an interesting method of divination using flowers. Seven factors are involved:

1. Asking a question
2. Choosing a flower
3. The day of the week in which the flower is at full bloom
4. The numerological day
5. The color of the flower
6. The numerological meaning of the flower
7. Interpreting the results

Asking a Question

You can ask questions on any subject at all. However, they must be serious in nature. Although you can ask questions for other people, the best results come when you ask about something that is important to you.

Choosing a Flower

For the purposes of this divination you need to choose a flower that is in full bloom on the day of the week that relates to your question. Each day of the week relates to a different type of question:

- Sunday: This is a good day for questions relating to finance, business, and monetary success.
- Monday: This is a good day for asking questions relating to health.
- Tuesday: This is a good day for asking questions that relate to problems and difficulties.
- Wednesday: This is a good day for questions relating to business matters and travel.
- Thursday: This is a good day for asking questions relating to psychic or spiritual concerns.
- Friday: This is a good day for questions relating to love and close relationships. This includes both marriage and divorce.

• Saturday: This is a good day for asking questions about matters that you find puzzling, mysterious, or intriguing.

Naturally, the choice of flower depends on the time of year. Obviously, in winter your choice will be more limited than in the summer months. You may feel that nothing flowers in the middle of winter. However, primrose, crocus and iris bloom in January, and tulips and Easter daisies can be found in February. If possible, choose a flower that you like and can easily identify.

Numerological Day

This is determined by adding up the total of the month, day and year in which you are performing this divination, and bringing it down to a single digit. Here's an example. Suppose you are doing this divination on August 12, 2006.

8 (month) + 1 + 2 (day) + 2 + 0 + 0 + 6 (year) = 19.
1 + 9 = 10, and 1 + 0 = 1.

August 12, 2006 is a 1 day numerologically.

Here is another example: January 3, 2007.

1 + 3 + 2 + 0 + 0 + 7 = 13, and 1 + 3 = 4.

January 3, 2007 is a 4 day numerologically.

Each personal day has a meaning:

• One Day. A good day for starting something new or for making changes. You will have plenty of enthusiasm, energy and good ideas.

- Two Day. A good day for close relationships and intuitive insights. You may need to be patient, as matters take their time on a Two Day.

- Three Day. A good day for social activities and having a good time. Light-hearted and frivolous activities are favored.

- Four Day. A good day for routine, everyday tasks. It is a day of hard work, but one that pays off, providing a great deal of personal satisfaction.

- Five Day. A day of change and variety. A good time to try something different or new. This is the day to finally do something you've been looking forward to.

- Six Day. A good day for home and family activities. All close relationships are favored.

- Seven Day. You will feel like spending at least some time on your own to get in touch with your inner nature, to learn, and to grow spiritually.

- Eight Day. A dynamic, progressive day with your abilities at their peak. A good day for all financial activities.

- Nine Day. A good day for re-evaluations and for making future plans. Emotions are heightened, and you may need to be understanding and compassionate.

Color of the Flower

The color of a flower is usually the first thing we notice. Everyone has personal preferences when it comes to flowers, and color is one of the more important factors. The color of the flower needs to be interpreted for the purposes of this divination.

White

A white flower symbolizes innocence, purity, virginity, trust, and honesty.

Red

A red flower symbolizes love, passion, strength, and courage.

Yellow

A yellow flower symbolizes generosity, good fortune, abundance, prosperity, and fertility.

Green

A green flower symbolizes hope, anticipation, and growth.

Blue

A blue flower symbolizes knowledge, wisdom, spirituality, and refinement.

Purple

A purple flower symbolizes ambition, power, attainment, and position.

Numerology for Flowers

The name of the flower is also important. In chapter 3 we discussed your personal colors according to numerology. We can use the same chart to determine the meanings of flowers. Here is the number/letter chart again:

1	2	3	4	5	6	7	8	9
A	B	C	D	E	F	G	H	I
J	K	L	M	N	O	P	Q	R
S	T	U	V	W	X	Y	Z	

Roses are always popular. Let's see what numerology has to say about them:

ROSE

9615 = 21, and 2 + 1 = 3. Rose has an Expression number of 3. Three is the number of fun, laughter, and expressing the joys of life.

However, rose also has a Soul Urge number of 11 (from the O and E). This means illumination, inspiration, and intuition.

Consequently, roses bring fun and laughter into our lives. In addition, they also open the door to our higher selves, allowing us to access our intuitions, as well as our most profound, illuminating, and inspirational thoughts.

Here is another example:

RHODODENDRON

9 8 6 4 6 4 5 5 4 9 6 5 = 71, and 7 + 1 = 8

The rhododendron is a powerful flower, which can potentially attract money and other material benefits. It has a Soul Urge of 5 (from the three Os and the E), which denotes freedom, variety, and change. 5 relates well to self-employment, making the humble rhododendron a good flower for people wanting to progress financially in their own business venture.

Interpreting the Results

Let's assume that you are attracted to someone and want to know if your feelings are reciprocated. The correct day for asking a question of this nature is Friday. You wait until Friday morning, and then ask: "Is . . . . in love with me?" You check in your diary and find that it is July 1, 2005. That is a 6 day.

You look for a flower that is in full bloom, and find a marigold. It seems appropriate as this plant was named after the Virgin Mary. It also has a beautiful yellow bloom.

The next step is to work out the numerological indications:

MARIGOLD
4 1 9 9 7 6 3 4 = 43, and 4 + 3 = 7. This is the Expression number for marigold. You work out the Soul Urge number and discover it is also a 7 (A, I, and O).

To summarize:

On Friday, July 1, 2005, you asked if a certain person was in love with you.

You chose a marigold, which is yellow. This is promising, as yellow relates to generosity, good fortune, and fertility. These are all potentially good traits in a relationship, especially if you ultimately want a family.

The date is propitious also, as the numerological day is a 6, which favors all close relationships.

However, the reading is not entirely positive, as marigold provides two 7s. Seven is reserved, introspective, and difficult to get to know.

This is a fairly typical outcome. When everything is positive, you know right away that the answer will be positive. However, most of the time you will receive a mixture of positive and negative indications, and will have to try to balance and reconcile them.

In this case, if the possible partner is introspective and difficult to get to know, the 7s will indicate him or her. If that is not the case, the 7s appear to indicate caution. You should get to know the other person a bit more first, and then ask the question again.

Flower Readings for Others

Reading flowers is a rather unusual psychic ability. You will not find it hard to find psychic readers who use tarot cards, palmistry or rune stones, but chances are you have never experienced a flower reading. Flower reading requires a considerable degree of intuition, as well as observation skills.

The person wanting a reading brings his or her own flower in a vase. This is to keep the flower as fresh as possible. The reader takes the flower out of the vase to give the reading. He or she examines the entire flower first, looking for signs that would escape most people.

The flower is read from the bottom of the stem to the top of the bloom. The bottom of the stem relates to the person's childhood. It is an indication of a difficult childhood if this area is torn or cut roughly. The opposite applies if the flower has been neatly cut.

The stalk represents the person's life until the present. The bloom represents the future. Any imperfections in the stalk, such as discolorations, thinning or twisting, indicate problem periods in the person's life. New branches indicate new beginnings, and leaves symbolize friends and family.

The bloom is looked at carefully to determine the subject's future. The choice of color and the fullness of the bloom are evaluated. A bud, rather than a bloom, indicates that a resolution to the subject's problem is still ahead. A bloom indicates a successful outcome, and a dying bloom shows that the outcome has already occurred, even if the subject is not yet aware of it.

The color usually provides a clue as to the nature of the sitter's problem:

- White: relates to trust
- Red: relates to love and passion
- Yellow and Orange: relate to financial matters
- Green: relates to hope, anticipation, and growth
- Blue: relates to knowledge and spirituality
- Purple: relates to ambition and power

You will not know if you have ability at this sort of reading until you try it. I believe that everyone possesses clairvoyant potential, although in most cases this natural ability is never developed. If you have been working on developing your psychic ability, you might find flower reading a useful way to take your skills to another level.

Your Personal Flower

There is a flower that relates to your Day of Birth reduced to a single number. Master numbers are not included in this. Consequently, 11 gets reduced down to a 2 (1 + 1 = 2) and 22 becomes a 4.

Birthday	Flower
1, 10, 19, 28	Lily
2, 11, 20, 29	Jasmine
3, 12, 21, 30	Lily of the Valley
4, 13, 22, 31	Bluebell
5, 14, 23	Gardenia
6, 15, 24	Rose
7, 16, 25	Lavender
8, 17, 26	Camellia
9, 18, 27	Rosemary

In addition to this, any flower with an Expression or Soul Urge number that relates to your Life Path, Expression, Soul Urge, or Day of Birth has a strong connection to you and can be considered "your" flower.

Colorful Dreams

People spend about a third of their lives asleep. About a quarter of that time—two hours a night—is spent dreaming. It seems that dreams are essential for good mental health. Yet many people claim that they never dream at all. This is because they forget their dreams almost as soon as they wake up. Dreams are often remembered as fragments that can be hard to understand. Consequently, most people pay little attention to them. This is a shame, as dreams can be a useful way to understand and make sense of our lives.

Some people seem to always dream in color, while others dream only in black and white. Still others have dreams that are sometimes in color and at other times in black and white. In fact, they may experience both in one night.

There are many theories about this. One is that people dream in color when they are unwell, and the significant colors provide an indication as to the nature of the illness. Another theory is that people dream in color when recalling their childhood, as everything is bright and colorful when looked at many years later. It's possible that colorful dreams are another form of symbolism. Instead of experiencing the symbolism as an object or experience, the message is revealed as a specific color. Unfortunately, no one has managed to come up with a solution that answers every possibility. Until someone does, enjoy all your dreams, regardless of whether or not they are in color.

Colors have symbolic meanings. If you wake up remembering a particular color featured in a dream, there is likely to be a reason for it. Sometimes this is obvious. You are likely to experience unpleasant colors in a nightmare, for instance. If you received a gold object in a dream, it is a clear sign that you will shortly be honored or recognized for something you have done. Here is a list of colors that may not be as easy to interpret.

Black

Black is an indication of obstacles. You are likely to feel frustrated or powerless, but must pursue your goal regardless of the indifference or interference of others.

Blue

Blue is an indication that you're progressing spiritually. You're prepared to cooperate with others and work for what is right and good. It's also a sign of happiness, security and love.

Brown

Brown is a sign of hard work. You will be called upon to work hard and long to achieve a specific task. You will wonder why you are doing it at times, but will ultimately be rewarded for your contribution.

Gold

Gold is a sign of ultimate success. It is a symbol of enlightenment, manifestation, and an indicator that you are on the right path.

Gray

Gray is a sign of doubt and uncertainty. You should pause and ask yourself if what you are doing is fair for everyone concerned.

Green

Green is a sign of spiritual, mental, emotional, and physical healing. You are being cleansed, and given an opportunity to make something of your life. Green creates harmony and contentment.

A dirty, muddy green is a sign of envy and hate.

Indigo

Indigo is an unusual color to recognize in a dream. It is a sign of clairvoyance and precognition, particularly concerning people who are close to you.

Orange

Orange is a sign of vitality and stimulation. It indicates a step forward in your career. However, an overabundance of orange indicates lust and pride.

Pink

Pink is an indication of love, tenderness, and sensitivity. It harmonizes and restores the soul. In a dream, pink can sometimes indicate a need for love.

Red

Red is a sign of power. It indicates energy, passion, drive, ambition, and integrity. Most of the time, red is a positive sign, but a dirty red indicates anger and aggression.

Silver

Silver is an indication of emotional coolness. It symbolizes secrets, hidden desires, and shifting alliances. It is a sign of intuition, but the results need to be evaluated carefully, as there is also the potential to fool oneself.

Violet

Violet is a sign of selflessness, spirituality, protection, and ultimate wisdom. It is an indication that you have released yourself from the desires of your lower self, have taken responsibility for your own life, and are moving forward in your own way.

White

White is a symbol of spirituality, inner peace, purity, and perfection. Large areas of white in a dream can indicate a rigid, disapproving approach to life.

Yellow

Yellow is a symbol of thought, intellect, and a desire to learn. This needs to be harnessed carefully, as there is a tendency to start many things, but to finish only a few. It is often an indication of a problem that will take a great deal of thought to resolve.

A muddy yellow is a sign of dishonesty and deceit.

Color Drawing

This is an interesting way to explore the symbolism of your dreams using color, even if you are certain that you only ever dream in black and white. This experiment works even if you find it hard to recall your dreams when you wake up.

Before going to bed, place an artist's pad and some colored pencils on your bedside table. When you wake up in the morning, before getting out of bed, reach over for the pad and pencils and draw anything that occurs to you, using the colors that feel right. It makes no difference what you draw. It can be abstract, realistic, cartoon-like, or just a few splotches of color. Once you have done this, get out of bed and get ready for your day. Do not think about what you created on the pad. Leave it until you have time to look at it later.

When you have a few spare minutes, sit down and look at what you produced. Try not to think about the quality of the work, but wait to see what impressions come into your mind. The first time I did this exercise, I drew a fir tree. It had a brown trunk, green foliage, and what looked like a red ball on the very top. It could have been a Christmas tree, waiting to be decorated. I was extremely unimpressed as it was the sort of tree I create when idly doodling. However, when I forgot about my lack of artistic skill and waited to see what came to me, I was surprised.

I was contemplating a new business venture at the time, and the tree seemed to indicate success. In fact, the sloping sides of the tree almost looked like stairs heading upward. I took this as a positive sign. Most trees are green, but all the same, the green appeared to indicate financial opportunity, and the red ball at the top seemed to indicate that I'd have the necessary motivation and persistence to reach it.

Even stranger was the fact that, while doing this, part of my dream came back to me. I hadn't remembered it when I woke up, but now my memory of it returned in vivid detail. In the dream, I was driving around a large city calling on potential customers. Everyone was saying no to whatever it was I was offering. However, it didn't matter. I was proud of my product and was not going to give up.

This also seemed to be an indication of success. Not surprisingly, after this experience, I investigated the opportunity more seriously and went ahead with it.

What do you do if you produce a shape rather than a picture? This, too, can be interpreted. Obviously your choice of color (or colors) has a meaning, and you should consider why you chose a particular color, instead of another. The shape can also be interpreted. Occasionally, you may produce a design that needs to be considered as two or three different symbols. Here are the meanings of the most common shapes:

- Square: A square symbolizes security, balance, good faith, and permanence.
- Circle: A circle symbolizes unity, wholeness, protection, and perfection.
- Triangle: A triangle symbolizes life, divinity, harmony, and prosperity.
- Star: A star symbolizes guidance, guardianship, high ideals, insight, and aspiration.
- Cross: A cross symbolizes crossroads, meaning a decision has to be made.
- Spiral: A spiral symbolizes cyclic development, indicating the ebbs and flows of life. It indicates that you should go with the flow, rather than fighting it.

Lucid Dreams

Most people have had the experience of becoming aware that they are dreaming while in the middle of a dream. This is known as lucid dreaming. Unfortunately, most people wake themselves up at this stage and miss the opportunity to gain valuable insights. Next time you find yourself lucid dreaming, consciously ask the dream to take you somewhere that will help you understand what is going on in your life at that time. Observe the scene as closely as possible. Notice as many details as possible, and pay special attention to the colors you see. Spend as long as you can in this scene before letting it go.

At this point you can wake yourself up, if you wish. Alternatively, you might want to return to your normal sleep. Either response is fine, as you will remember your lucid dream when you wake up.

If possible, think about your dream before getting out of bed. When you get up, make notes about the experience, including the colors you saw. See if you can recapture the feelings you experienced in the dream. You may receive some insights as you do this. If so, write them down as well. Later in the day, when you have time, relax quietly, read through your notes, and see what information has come through. At times it will be obvious, but sometimes you will need to search for the message. This is when your knowledge of color will prove most helpful. Look at the major objects in the dream and focus on their colors. You will gradually become aware of the symbols and themes that crop up regularly in your dreams.

You may not want to wait until you happen to have a lucid dream. Fortunately, there are methods to help encourage them. The method I find most helpful is to set an alarm clock to go off four hours after I've gone to bed. That wakes me enough to turn it off, and I can then go back to sleep and return to the dream I was having. Once I am back inside the dream, I can then direct it to go anywhere I wish.

Another method is to tell yourself before falling asleep that you will experience a lucid dream during the night. It is best to ask for a lucid dream on the weekend, or at some other time when you do not have to leap out of bed and start your day. This is because the most valuable time to think about your dreams is when you first wake up. Waking up to an alarm clock does not give you enough time to think about your dreams. This is why so many dreams are forgotten within minutes of getting out of bed.

A third method is to regularly tell yourself that whenever you see, say, your hand in a dream, you will immediately become aware that you are dreaming and will be able to direct it.

A method that many people find useful is when you wake up early remembering the dream you have just experienced. Relax quietly and see if you can return to the dream. Once you are inside it again, you can start taking it wherever you want to go.

None of these methods works every time. I am always delighted to experience a lucid dream, but have learned not to be concerned when it fails to happen. I know that next time, or the time after, I'll be able to enjoy another lucid dream.

National Emblems

It can be an interesting exercise to look at national flags and try to work out the symbolism of the various colors and other features. Some are obvious. Crosses tend to indicate Christian countries, while crescents indicate Islamic nations. A hammer and sickle clearly indicate communism.

Flags date back to the ancient Egyptians and Assyrians who used sacred objects mounted on poles to symbolize royal authority and to serve as rallying points in battle. Heraldry became a serious art in the twelfth century, and this had a major influence on the design and symbology of flags. The study of the history, symbolism, design, and other aspects of flags is called vexillology.

Just recently, someone told me an interesting piece of trivia about the flags used by the countries involved in World Wars I and II. In WWI, France, Great Britain, and the United States all had flags containing red, white and blue. Incidentally, so did Russia until it made a separate peace and changed the color of their flag to red. However, not one of the Central Powers had flags containing red, white, and blue.

In WWII, France, Great Britain, and the United States were involved again. The Netherlands and Norway were also involved. They all had flags containing red, white, and blue. Again, not one of the opposing Axis Powers had flags containing red, white, and blue.

Some people might dismiss this as simply coincidence, but it makes me think that the combination of red, white, and blue might possess some sort of psychic or mystical power.

Your Personal Protective Shield

You are probably familiar with heraldic shields. Usually, they consist of two to four colors, all of which have specific meanings. In my classes, I often encouraged my students to create an abstract picture using specific colors that appealed to them. One of my students was studying heraldry, and arrived at the class a week later with a beautiful shield he had made using his personal colors. A shield is a form of protection, and this made me realize that the artwork could be much, much more than a picture made up of favorite colors.

As a result, since then, I have suggested to my students that they create a picture, or a shield, that feels protective. Whenever they feel the need for strength or protection, all they need do is look at their picture for a few seconds, and they will feel calm and protected.

Use the color symbolism from this chapter, along with your personal colors and colors that appeal to you, to create a picture that inspires you and also feels protective. Once you have done this, display it somewhere in your home and use it whenever necessary.

CHAPTER ELEVEN

COLOR AND MAGIC

Magic is the ability to exert change on the world using the power of your mind. In other words, it is the ability to attract whatever it is you want. You need to clearly focus on a specific goal until it becomes manifested in your life. If you can clearly visualize something in your mind, you have the ability to make it become a reality. One definition of magic that I have always liked is by Florence Farr, one of the leading members of the Hermetic Order of the Golden Dawn. She wrote: "Magic consists of removing the limitations from what we think are the earthly and spiritual laws that bind or compel us. We can be anything because we are All."[1]

Magic is not wishful thinking. Concentration, clear focus, and energy are added to the visualization to create the necessary power for the magic to occur.

Obviously, it is vitally important that your magic does not hurt others in any way. There is a traditional belief that any magic performed with a negative or destructive intent will rebound threefold against the magician. This is known as the Threefold Law of Return. It is worth bearing this in mind when contemplating any form of magic. Negative magic is called black magic, and beneficial magic is termed white magic. Gray magic lives between these two extremes. Although magic has been defined in colorful terms, magic is actually neutral and colorless. It should go without saying that all of your magic should be white magic, and performed for the good of everyone concerned.

There is a tendency for people to think that magic can solve all their problems. Consequently, they immediately perform a magic spell or ritual whenever something goes wrong in their life. In fact, magic should be used only as a last resort. Try to resolve your problems in a nonmagical way first, and use magic only when those methods fail to produce the desired results.

Color magic involves four steps:

1. Deciding on your goal.

2. Determining which element your goal belongs to.

3. Determining the right colors for the ritual.

4. Performing the magic ritual.

Choosing Your Goal

There is little point in performing magic unless you have a specific goal in mind. This could be anything at all. Your goal might be something specifically for you, or it might be intended to help humanity as a whole. It makes no difference what it is, as long as it hurts no one.

First of all, you need to determine if your aim is something that you can achieve by normal means. Let's assume, for example, that you want a raise at work. There are many ways to achieve this particular goal. You might make yourself so useful and conscientious at work that your boss might increase your pay without any need for you to ask. This method may or may not work, depending on your boss and the corporation you work for. Another method would be to ask your boss for a pay raise. This is more likely to work if you have a specific sum in mind, and can justify the pay raise with a list of what you have achieved. Let's assume that you have tried both of these methods without success. At this stage you have two obvious choices: you start looking for another position that pays the amount of money you feel you deserve, or you continue your job at the same salary as before. Fortunately, there is another possibility: magic. If the other methods fail to produce the desired result, you should pause and think about why you did not receive the pay increase you deserved. There might be reasons that are totally unrelated to you and your ability. You might, for instance, already be earning the maximum amount of money that your particular job pays. It is possible that the corporation might not be able to afford to pay you any more at present. Fortunately, after doing this assessment, if you still feel you deserve the pay increase, you could create a magic ritual to attract to you the increase that you deserve. The magic is performed as the final step, not the first.

The Four Elements

You have chosen a goal. The second step is to decide which element is most relevant to your goal.

Thousands of years ago, our ancestors tried to make sense of the world and came to the conclusion that everything was composed of Earth, Water, Air, and Fire. The Sicilian-born Greek philosopher Empedocles (c. 490–430 B.C.E.), was the first to record these principles in his book *On Nature*. He believed that nothing either came into existence, or ceased to exist, and that everything was in a state of change caused by love and strife. The interactions of these two forces created the elements of Earth, Water, Air, and Fire. A century later, Aristotle (384–322 B.C.E.) added ether as a fifth element.

Plato (c. 428–347 B.C.E.) felt that the four elements were completely intertwined, as they could easily pass from one to another. He wrote: "Let us begin with what we now call water. We see it, or we suppose, solidifying into stones and earth, and again dissolving and evaporating into wind and air."[2] Consequently, he felt that the four elements should be considered as qualities that reflect their essential natures.

The four elements can still be regarded as qualities, principles, and forces today, and a huge number of associations have been attached to them. Naturally, these also include colors. Here is a list of a few of the associations attached to each element:

Air

Temperament: Sanguine

Attribute: Intellectual, fun-loving

Function: Thought

Direction: East

Season: Spring

Archangel: Raphael

Elementals: Sylphs

Tarot suit: Wands

Playing card suit: Clubs

Signs of the Zodiac: Gemini, Libra, Aquarius

Color (active): Orange, Yellow

Color (passive): Violet

Fire

Temperament: Choleric

Attribute: Spiritual, enthusiastic

Function: Intuition

Direction: South

Season: Summer

Archangel: Michael

Elementals: Salamanders

Tarot suit: Swords

Playing card suit: Spades
Signs of the Zodiac: Aries, Leo, Sagittarius
Color (active): Red
Color (passive): Green

Water

Temperament: Phlegmatic
Attribute: Feeling, nurturing
Function: Emotion
Direction: West
Archangel: Gabriel
Elementals: Undines
Tarot suit: Cups
Playing card suit: Hearts
Signs of the Zodiac: Cancer, Scorpio, Pisces
Season: Autumn
Color (active): White, Blue
Color (passive): Black

Earth

Temperament: Melancholic
Attribute: Physical, security
Function: Touch
Direction: North
Archangel: Uriel
Elementals: Gnomes
Tarot suit: Pentacles
Playing card suit: Diamonds
Signs of the Zodiac: Taurus, Virgo, Capricorn

Season: Winter
Color (active): Yellow, Green
Color (passive): Blue

You can use the four elements in a number of ways to enhance your color magic. Your magic will become much more powerful once you decide which element your goal belongs to. Once you have determined this, you can use objects and colors that relate to the particular element. In practice, your magic will use all four elements, but the predominant one should be determined by your specific goal.

Here is a list of goals that relate to the different elements:

Air: (Independence, Intellect, Positivity)
Addictions
All forms of Communication
Awareness
Creativity
Education
Knowledge
Travel
Writing

Fire: (Courage, Power, Spirituality)
Change
Competition
Creativity
Health
Legal matters
Loyalty

Sex
Spirituality
Sports
Success

Water: (Compassion, Feelings, Tranquility)
Children
Emotions
Family
Friendships
Healing
Home
Intuition
Love
Reason

Earth: (Endurance, Material Success, Responsibility)
Abundance
Agriculture
Career
Investments
Money
Property
Prosperity
Wisdom

Another way of selecting the correct element for your magic is to look at them this way:

- Use Fire if you need vitality and energy
- Use Earth if you need stability
- Use Air if you need encouragement and support
- Use Water if you wish to dissolve or eliminate something

Choosing the Correct Color

You now have a goal and have determined which element it belongs to. The element will have provided you with a color, but you also need to choose a color that relates to your specific goal. Here are some possibilities:

White

You can use white for any goal. It cleanses, purifies, clarifies, and heals. Use white whenever you have doubts about what color you should use.

Red

You should use red if your goal relates to courage, strength, sex, or major changes. Men should use red for any sexual problems.

Orange

You should use orange if your goal relates to creativity or you are seeking a more positive future. Women should use orange to help overcome any sexual problems.

Yellow

You should use yellow if your goal relates to study or other intellectual pursuits. It should also be used for goals relating to communication. It can also be used to attract like-minded friends and to create an enjoyable environment.

Green

Green is the perfect color for healing and financial increase. It also eases difficult situations and helps provide persistence and staying power.

Blue

You should use blue if your goal relates to loyalty, trust, and honesty. It encourages clear thinking and dissipates anger and other negative emotions.

Indigo

You should use indigo if your goal relates to home and family matters. It resolves difficulties between family members and enhances love and contentment.

Purple

You should use purple if your goal involves spiritual endeavors or any activity intended to benefit humanity as a whole. Purple also relieves tension between friends.

Pink

You should use pink to attract close relationships and to nurture yourself on an emotional level.

Black

Black absorbs negative energy and should be used only when you feel surrounded by negativity and can see no way out. Burn a black candle for one hour every night until it has burned away. After that, you can start working with a colored candle that symbolizes your goal.

Creating and Performing a Magical Ritual

The final stage is to send your desire out into the universe where it will be acted upon. If your goal relates to increase, you should perform the ritual while the moon is waxing (growing). If you are performing the ritual to remove something from your life, you should perform the ritual while the moon is waning (decreasing).

You can also work your magic on specific days of the week that relate to the color of your goal:

Monday: White

Tuesday: Red

Wednesday: All colors

Thursday: Blue

Friday: Green

Saturday: Black

Sunday: Yellow

Gather together the objects that you will need to conduct the ritual. Think about the element or elements you wish to make most use of in the ritual. Here are some suggestions:

Fire: Candles, and any small red objects

Air: Incense, feathers, freshly picked fragrant flowers, and any small yellow objects

Water: Water and any small blue objects

Earth: Crystals, stones, pottery, and any small green objects

You will also need a quiet space where you will not be disturbed. In warm weather, I prefer to perform my rituals outdoors. Naturally, in cold or inclement weather, I perform them indoors.

You will need a magic circle to perform your ritual within. You can draw a circle on the ground or indicate it in some other way. I have a circular rug that I use when working indoors. If you do not wish to create a physical circle, you can imagine it instead. The easiest way to do this is to stand in the center of where your imaginary circle will be. Face east, and slowly turn around in a clockwise direction with your right arm and first and second fingers extended. Visualize protective energy flowing down your arm and out through your fingers to cast a circle of protection.

If you wish, you can use the element that relates to your goal to create your magic circle. If this is the Earth element, use stones, rocks, crystal, or salt to outline your circle. Start facing the east, and move in a clockwise direction. If the element is Water, start in the east and move around in a circle, sprinkling water on the ground to indicate the perimeter. If the element is Air, walk around the perimeter with incense. Do exactly the same with a lit candle if the element is Fire.

The circle is important as it protects you from harm while performing your magic. It also keeps the magical energy you have created inside the circle until you are ready to release it. Consequently, once you are inside the circle, you should stay there until your ritual has been completed.

You might decide to use an altar to hold the objects you will be using. A small table or stool is ideal for this, especially if you cover it with a cloth of the correct color for the magic you are performing. I position the altar so that I face east while working at it. Some people prefer to face north, and this is a matter of personal preference.

Place everything you will need during the ritual on the altar. You might have candles, incense, crystals, a container of water, and other objects that relate to your request. If you are seeking more money, for instance, you might place several dollar bills on your altar, as they keep your mind firmly fixed on your purpose in conducting the ritual. Photographs or drawings of your goal work in exactly the same way. I usually create an outline of the ritual and place a copy of this on the altar to keep me on track.

You should also have a small object that is the same color as the element your request relates to. This might be a small ornament that you can display in your home afterward, or something smaller, such as a crystal or photograph that you can carry in a purse or pocket. In the course of the ritual, these objects will become imbued with the energy created by the circle and your ritual. Each time you see or hold them, their color reminds of the ritual, and this adds additional power to your request.

If possible, you should bathe before entering the circle. A leisurely bath is preferable to a shower, as it enables you to relax completely. You can also involve all four elements in the process. Obviously, the water in the bath supplies the Water element. You can also burn candles to provide Fire, and incense for the Air element. Bath salts provide Earth.

After your bath, dry yourself and get ready for the ritual. Wear clean, loose-fitting clothes. Some magicians prefer to work skyclad (naked). Again, this is a personal choice.

Step into your circle and face east. This is the direction of the Air element. If you have performed magic before, you may have started the ritual by invoking the four archangels (Raphael, Michael, Gabriel, and Uriel), as they rule the four directions. If you have worked with them before, you may prefer to start by calling on the archangels before visualizing the colors. The same thing applies with any other method of starting a ritual. If a certain method is comfortable and appealing to you, you should use it.

However, this is not essential, and you will be successful even if you have never worked magic before. For the purposes of color magic, you can start by visualizing the colors that relate to each direction.

Point to the east, with the first two fingers of your right hand extended. Visualize a small circle of pure yellow at the level of your right hand, on the perimeter of the magic circle. Allow this to gradually grow until a quarter of your magic circle consists of pure yellow energy, directly in front of you. Some people are able to actually "see" the color, but others sense that it is there. Once you are aware that the yellow is looking after this quadrant of the circle, thank it for protecting you. You might say: "Element of Air, I salute you and thank you for your help in my request."

Turn to face south, which is the Fire direction. Visualize the color red in the same way as you did with the yellow, and allow it to grow until it also fills up a quarter of the perimeter of your circle. Sense that it is connected to the yellow, and that you now have a semicircle of protection. Thank the Fire element for its help, and then turn to the west. Visualize the color blue, and give thanks to the element of Water. Finally, face north and visualize green, the color of Earth.

Once you have given thanks to the Earth element, turn to face east again. You are now completely surrounded by a circle of protection. You might like to confirm this by looking around and sensing the circle of protection that you have created. You might "see" this as a huge wall painted in four different colors. You might see it as a mist, with colors inside it. One lady I know visualizes it as a large circular hedge, with invisible lights that provide the four colors. Many years ago, a man told me that he imagined himself inside a giant igloo, divided into quarters of different colors. I was impressed with what he said, as the magic circle is much more than a line on the ground or a wall of energy.

The magic circle completely surrounds you in every direction, and can be visualized as a bubble of protective energy, much like an igloo. As you can see, different people "see" the protection in varying ways. It makes no difference how you sense the circle of protection and the four colors, as long as you know that they are there.

It is now time to make your request. Focus on the object that belongs to the same element as your request. This might be a candle, if your request relates to the Fire element. Light the candle before picking it up. Hold the candle at about chest height and tell it exactly what you want. There is no need to use formal language. Speak to it using the same words that you use when talking with a friend. Once you have done this, replace the candle on your altar or on the ground. Watch the smoke spiralling upward and visualize it going out into the universe to make your desires a reality.

If your request relates to the Air element, you are likely to be using incense, feathers, and/or flowers. Again tell the objects what you desire. Visualize the smoke of the incense going out into the universe. If you are using a feather, hold it in your cupped hands while talking to it, and then carry it with you until your request has become a reality. If you are using flowers, talk to them, and then place them somewhere where you will see them regularly. Each time you see them, your desire will come to your mind, and this further reinforces your desire on the universe.

If your request relates to the Earth element, you may like to use a crystal. Hold the crystal in your cupped hands while talking to it, and then keep it with you until your desire becomes a reality. Hold the crystal at least once a day, and think about your goal for a few moments.

If the element is Water, you will need a glass of water. Hold the glass and talk to the water, telling it about your desire. This is called "magnetizing" the water, as you are charging it with your desire. Once you have done this, mentally bless the water, and then drink it.

The final step of your ritual is to give thanks to the universe for making your request a reality. You do this as if your request has already been accomplished. You can now close your circle. The easiest way to do this is to thank all four directions, starting in the east and moving in a counterclockwise direction. Moving to the left, rather than the right, is called "widdershins." Sense the four colors again as you do this, and offer a sincere thanks to each of them. You may feel the circle gradually dissolving as you move in the widdershins direction.

Carefully extinguish any candles or incense that you may have used. Eat or drink something to help ground you again. Spend a few minutes relaxing and thinking about what you have achieved before carrying on with your day.

You should repeat the ritual at least once a week until your request has become a reality in your life.

Flashing Tablets

Flashing tablets are used for meditation. They consist of designs made from two complementary colors that create an optical illusion. When you gaze at them, the design appears to flash from one color to the other. They also create an intriguing after-image if you close your eyes after staring at them for a few minutes. You have probably experienced the sensation of gazing at a colored image for a length of time, and then looking at a white wall and seeing the image you were staring at outlined in a complementary color. Flashing tablets provide that effect without the need to look at a white wall or screen. Consequently, if you gaze at the red area of a flashing tablet that is, say, red and green, for any length of time, the muscles of your eyes will relax slightly, which changes their focus. This means you will suddenly "see" the complementary green color for a second. The red will then appear to flash in front of your eyes, and you start seeing surrealistic flashes of red and green. This sensation is hypnotic and creates a state that enables you to contact your subconscious mind.

Almost any combination of shapes painted in two complementary colors will create the necessary effect. In addition, there are specific colors and designs for each element:

Air: An orange circle inside a square of violet

Fire: A red triangle inside a square of green

Water: A white crescent moon inside a square of black

Earth: A yellow square inside a larger square of blue

Each symbol is placed inside a square, which symbolizes the Earth element. That is why the flashing tablet for Earth consists of a square inside a square. The other symbols relate to the mental world, and they are enclosed within a square to contain it inside a physical plane.

You will find it helpful to make flashing tablets to symbolize each element. You can use the tablet containing the element that most relates to your purpose to help you enter the desired state in order to clearly visualize your goal and send it out to the universe.

My tablets are twelve inches square. I have used smaller ones, but find that twelve inches is a good size. I used acrylic paint. Once the paint was dry I applied a clear varnish. This protects the tablets and provides an attractive, glossy surface.

You will need to experiment with the placement of your tablets. I find the perfect distance for me is to have the tablet about three feet away from my face, in a position where I can gaze at the center of the tablet without raising or lowering my head or eyes. This also depends on the size of your tablets.

Once you have discovered the right distance for you, all you need do is relax comfortably and gaze at the center of the tablet. After a few minutes you will experience one of two possibilities. Your eyes may start to feel heavy. If this occurs, close your eyes and notice the aftereffect created by the tablet. You will also find yourself in a relaxed, meditative state. You may even sense that you are inside the element that you are working with. If this occurs, pause and see if any clairvoyant insights occur to you. When you feel ready, think about your goal, and mentally send it out to the universe. The other possibility is that the colors of your tablet will start flashing. This may prove disorienting for a moment. Keep staring at the tablet for another sixty seconds, observing this fascinating effect. When you feel ready, close your eyes and enjoy the aftereffect. Pause for a minute or two to see what information comes to you. When you feel ready, start thinking about your goal, and consciously send it out to the universe confident that it will be acted upon.

As you have seen, color is of prime importance in magic. It would be hard to find anything more colorful and beautiful than crystals. Not surprisingly, they have always played a role in magic. We have already mentioned them briefly in chapter five, and will examine them more closely in the next chapter.

CHAPTER TWELVE

CRYSTALS AND GEMSTONES

Crystals and gemstones have been used for magical purposes since at least the time of the ancient Egyptians. Even then, people told stories about how the priests in Atlantis harnessed the power of gemstones and used it to communicate over long distances, and even to fly. Thousands of years ago, people were fascinated with the mystery, rarity, and natural beauty of crystals and gemstones. They have been revered and treasured ever since. This fascination has inspired many legends and stories about the powers and properties of precious stones.

The story of the Valley of Diamonds is a good example. It dates back some 2,500 years and appears in a number of forms in the myths and legends of different cultures. Apparently, there was a huge, deep gorge north of the Black Sea. Hideous snakes and terrifying eagles guarded it. Their task was to protect the huge quantity of diamonds that lay at the bottom of the gorge. A powerful king sent some of his servants to fetch the diamonds. The servants thought the task was impossible, but they finally came up with a good idea. They killed a number of sheep and cut them into quarters, which they threw into the gorge. The eagles flew down and gathered up the surprise feast and took it back to their nests. Diamonds stuck to the meat, and a day or two later, the servants raided the eagles' nests and retrieved the diamonds, which they were able to take back to their master.

Gemstones have been used as protective amulets for thousands of years, and are still frequently used for this purpose today. Crystal energy can help people to cure illnesses, enhance their intuition, cleanse and balance their chakras, develop spiritually, divine the future, and provide protection.

People collect gemstones for many reasons. Some people buy them because they are colorful and look attractive. Others collect stones that relate to their zodiac sign, or want stones that relate to each of the chakras. Some people use stones when meditating or divining the future. A lady I knew in Scotland placed gemstones on window ledges to protect her home. Color healers frequently collect stones that they can use to help heal others. Most people find their first stone by accident. It might be a gift, or perhaps they are attracted by its color or texture. Once they have one stone, it usually doesn't take long before several more have been added, and a collection is born.

Even if you don't have a crystal store in your neighborhood, the chances are high that someone will have stones for sale. Check the Yellow Pages under Crystals, Lapidaries and Minerals, and ask a local jeweller if he can recommend someone who sells loose gemstones. Ask at new age stores and health shops for people who sell gemstones from their homes, or at craft fairs or swap meets.

I believe that my gemstones have all chosen me, rather than the other way around. This is because I have frequently gone into a place that sells crystals and gemstones with the intention of buying a certain gemstone. However, I usually leave with two or three gemstones that were not on my list, and may not have bought the object I went in to buy. I am sure you will experience this, too, when you start looking at crystals and gemstones.

Take your time in choosing suitable gemstones. Every stone produces a different vibration that gives it its own unique feel. This is called "piezoelectricity." You will like the feel of some gemstones more than others. I always buy gemstones that feel right for me, even if I have no immediate use for them.

Sometimes you may feel nothing when you hold a certain gemstone. When this occurs, hold the gemstone loosely in your fist, close your eyes, and silently ask: "Are you the right stone for me?" You will feel a distinct positive or negative response.

Look at the stones carefully before buying them. You want the best stones you can afford. Consequently, you should avoid anything with noticeable imperfections. This is particularly the case with crystals. If you are buying a number of stones that will be used together, such as in chakra balancing or divination, you should look for stones that are similar in size and quality.

Choosing Your Crystals and Gemstones

Sometimes I deliberately search for a specific stone, or may have a color in mind. At other times, my choice is more random. I will browse in a gemstone store and see what stones attract my attention. I like to hold any stones that appeal to me to see if this is confirmed by psychometry. Often I'll arrive home with stones that I had no intention of buying a few hours earlier. Here are some of the more common stones that work well with color magic.

Red Stones

Bloodstone
Coral
Garnet
Red Jasper
Ruby
Sardonyx

Orange Stones
Carnelian
Cinnamon Aventurine
Fire Opal
Orange Calcite

Yellow Stones
Amber
Citrine
Yellow Sapphire
Topaz

Green Stones
Aventurine
Emerald
Jade
Malachite
Peridot

Blue Stones
Aquamarine
Chalcedony
Chrysocolla
Lapis Lazuli
Turquoise

Indigo Stones
Azurite
Indigo Sodalite
Iolite

Violet Stones
Amethyst
Fluorite
Purple Garnet
Sugilite

White Stones
Clear Quartz
Diamond
Moonstone
White Topaz

Pink Stones
Kunzite
Pink Coral
Pink Topaz
Rose Quartz
Rubelite (Pink Tourmaline)

Black Stones
Black Tourmaline
Hematite
Jet
Obsidian

Cleansing Your Crystals and Gemstones

Once you have bought your crystals and gemstones they will need to be cleansed before use. This is because they may have picked up negative energy before reaching you.

If you are using your stones regularly, you should cleanse them about once a week.

Cleansing is done using one of the four elements.

Cleansing with Water

The easiest way to cleanse your crystals and gemstones is to hold them under clean, running water for about thirty seconds and then allow them to dry in the sunlight. A stream or river is ideal for this. Seawater is also extremely good; this is a method I use frequently as I live close to the sea. Hold the gemstone under the water for about thirty seconds, and then let it dry naturally.

If you do not have a stream, river, or ocean nearby, you can add salt to rainwater and leave the gemstones in this solution overnight. Do not use tap water. Use bottled water if rainwater is not available.

You can create a small ritual to use while cleansing your stones. I usually say: "I am cleansing you so you can work at your peak at all times. Thank you for being prepared to help me in my aims."

Timing is an individual matter, too. A Cancerian lady I know always cleanses her crystals in moonlight, as the Moon is the ruler of her sign. Many people believe that the Moon cleanses, but the Sun energizes. You might prefer to cleanse your crystals in the evening and then allow them to dry overnight in the moonlight.

Cleansing with Earth

Crystals come from the earth, and relate to the Earth element. Consequently, many people believe that they should also be cleansed with earth. To do this, all you need do is bury your crystals and gemstones in earth for three nights. Say a few words as you bury them. I like to cleanse them in my garden. If you do not have a garden, the soil around a potted plant will work just as well.

Alternatively, you can bury them in a container of salt. Remember to dispose of the salt afterwards, as it will have picked up any negativity from the crystals and stones.

Cleansing with Fire

Cleansing with fire can be a convenient method, as you can do it before or after any ritual that involves candles. Hold the crystal or gemstone in your cupped hands while gazing into the flame of the candle. When you feel ready, look at the crystal or gemstone and speak to it before passing the stone through the flame. The stone must go through the flame rather than the smoke. You need to be careful not to burn yourself as you do this. Check the stone afterward. If there is no residue on it, it is ready for use. However, if there is any soot or dirt on it, you will need to rinse it in running water before using it.

Cleansing with Air

Cleansing with air is very convenient if you need to cleanse a stone and work with it right away. Hold the stone between the thumb and first finger of your nondominant hand (left hand if you are right-handed, and right hand if you are left-handed).

Take several slow deep breaths, and visualize yourself surrounded by pure, white light. Talk to the stone and then take another deep breath. Gently exhale cleansing white energy onto the stone. Turn the stone slightly between your fingers and repeat until every part of the stone has received pure white energy.

Charging Your Crystals and Gemstones

Once you have cleansed your crystals and gemstones, they need to be charged with positive energy to make them as effective as possible. A simple meditation is a quick and effective way to do this. Sit down comfortably somewhere where you will not be disturbed. Hold your stone between your clasped palms, close your eyes and take several slow deep breaths. Visualize yourself surrounded by a pure white light. Feel it in every cell of your body. Become aware of the crystal between your palms and send it thoughts of love. Continue sending love to the crystal until you feel a response. Thank it for being willing to help you. Squeeze the crystal slightly with your hands, and then open your eyes.

If you are not in a hurry, you can charge your crystal by placing it in a sunny spot for a few days. Alternatively, if you own a large crystal cluster, you can place your new crystal on this for a few days to allow it to absorb energy from the cluster and become charged that way.

Dedicating Your Crystal or Gemstone

The final part of the preparation stage is to dedicate your gemstone or crystal for the task it is to undertake. If you will be using your crystals for healing work, they will need to be dedicated to that purpose. Likewise, if you will be using them for divinatory purposes, they must be dedicated to provide the best readings possible. In time, you will probably find you have crystals dedicated to a variety of purposes. If you have several gemstones or crystals that need to be dedicated to the same purpose, you can dedicate them all at the same time.

Stand facing east, with the stone or stones in your clasped hands. Raise your hands as high as you can, and say, preferably out loud: "I dedicate you to help me (meditate, balance my chakras, heal others, divine the future, etc.). I empower you to work for the best interests of everyone involved. You are a force for good."

Bring your clasped hands down to chest level and hold them at the level of your heart chakra. Press the thumbs of your clasped hands against your chest, and thank the gemstone or crystal for agreeing to help you.

Your stone is now ready for use. You should repeat this exercise whenever you feel it is necessary. If you decide at a later stage to use the stone for some other purpose it will need to be rededicated.

You should treat your crystals and gemstones with care and respect. Allow them to receive plenty of sunlight. Stones that will be used for meditation and divinatory purposes should receive plenty of moonlight, also. It is not a good idea to keep your crystals and gemstones shut away in a drawer. Place them on a window ledge or shelf where they can receive sunlight and fresh air.

Stress Reduction

Gemstones and crystals play a valuable role in color healing. However, they can also be used to attain and maintain emotional and mental health. Stress is a major factor in problems of this sort.

Someone once said that the only people without stress are in graveyards. There is some truth in this, as we need a certain amount of stress to face life and achieve our goals. However, there is both good and bad stress.

If you feel tense, worried, or stressed, the most beneficial thing you can do is to remove yourself temporarily from the situation you are in and relax. Meditation is a good way of doing this, especially if you meditate with a stone that has been dedicated to healing. There are a number of stones that are believed to alleviate stress. These include: agate, amethyst, azurite, celestite, chrysoprase, garnet, kunzite, lepidolite, rose quartz, and tourmaline.

You will need a comfortable, warm place where you will not be disturbed. Play gentle background music if you wish. Sit or lie down comfortably, with the stone you have chosen in your nondominant hand. Relax all the muscles of your body. Once you feel completely relaxed, visualize the most peaceful scene you can imagine. This can be literally anywhere. You might choose to mentally visit a place you already know, or you may imagine a peaceful, calm, and tranquil scene. Enjoy this scenario for as long as you can. Do not try to hang on to it once it starts to fade.

Now it is time to focus on the stone or crystal in the palm of your hand. You might want to move your fingers to gently massage the stone. Become aware of the protective, healing energy the stone provides. Thank it for the help it is providing.

Enjoy the pleasant relaxation for as long as you wish. When you feel ready, take three slow, deep breaths and open your eyes. If possible, carry the stone you used around with you during the day. Touch it as often as possible, especially when you are tense or stressed. Expose it to sunlight regularly, and recharge it whenever necessary.

You can also strap it to your left wrist or place it under your pillow when you go to bed at night to enjoy the benefits the stone provides twenty-four hours a day.

You can use the same methods for a variety of problems. Here are some suggestions:

- Anger: Kyonite, Lapis Lazuli
- Apathy: Red Opal
- Depression: Emerald, Lapis Lazuli, Tourmaline, Turquoise
- Emotional blocks: Fire Agate, Fire Opal, Obsidian, Tiger-Eye
- Clarity (increasing): Amethyst, Aquamarine, Azurite

- Compassion (developing): Jade, Rhodochrosite
- Concentration: Amethyst, Fluorite, Sugilite, Tiger-Eye
- Confidence: Citrine, Lapis Lazuli, Rose Quartz
- Confusion: Diamond, Fluorite, Rhodonite, Selenite
- Courage: Agate, Bloodstone, Rhodonite, Sardonyx
- Depression: Agate, Green Tourmaline
- Desperation: Rubellite, Smoky Quartz
- Egoism: Amethyst, Rhodochrosite
- Emotional balance: Chalcedony, Kunzite, Moonstone
- Emotional outbursts: Amethyst, Chrysoprase
- Energy: Garnet, Quartz, Ruby
- Envy: Ruby
- Fear: Amethyst, Citrine, Rose Quartz
- Frustration: Opal, Peridot
- Grief: Amethyst, Peridot, Quartz
- Insomnia: Amethyst, Rose Quartz
- Introversion: Lapis Lazuli, Tourmaline
- Intuition: Moonstone
- Jealousy: Diamond
- Melancholy: Aventurine, Kunzite, Peridot
- Negativity: Tourmaline
- Nervous exhaustion: Diamond, Gold Topaz
- Overcaution: Chrysoprase, Heliotrope
- Pessimism: Rose Quartz, Smoky Quartz

- Sadness: Amethyst, Diamond, Lepidolite
- Self-discipline: Azurite, Dolomite, Lapis Lazuli
- Self-esteem: Alexandrite, Garnet
- Shyness: Lapis Lazuli, Rhodochrosite, Rose Quartz
- Stress: Aventurine, Beryl, Chrysocolla, Jasper

Prosperity Stones

When I first started speaking about crystals and gemstones, I was surprised at the number of people who wanted crystals to attract wealth and abundance. I had been expecting people to inquire about love, spiritual growth, intuition, and health, rather than money. Fortunately, I was able to answer these requests, as there are specific stones that can be used to attract abundance, in every sense of the word, to us.

There are both general prosperity stones and specific prosperity stones that relate to your Life Path number in numerology. General prosperity stones that can be carried by anyone to attract wealth and abundance are: Alexandrite, Amethyst, Citrine, Diamond, Jade, Clear Quartz, Ruby, Sapphire, and Topaz. People have worn these particular stones for thousands of years to attract prosperity.

Your specific prosperity stone is determined by your Life Path number, which you worked out in chapter 3. (It is your full date of birth, reduced down to a single digit, except for 11 and 22.)

- Life Path 1: Ruby
- Life Path 2: Carnelian

- Life Path 3: Yellow Citrine
- Life Path 4: Emerald
- Life Path 5: Sodalite
- Life Path 6: Azurite
- Life Path 7: Amethyst
- Life Path 8: Rose Quartz
- Life Path 9: Tiger-Eye
- Life Path 11: Hematite
- Life Path 22: Gold Topaz

You should carry prosperity stones close to your skin. Allow them to receive plenty of sunlight. At least once a day, hold your prosperity stone in your hand while saying positive affirmations. Affirmations consist of phrases that you repeat to yourself over and over again, to instill the thought in your mind. They are always phrased in the present tense, as if you already possessed the quality you were seeking. It is best to create your own affirmations. However, here are a few to get you started:

> *I create wealth and abundance.*
> *I gratefully accept my share from an abundant universe.*
> *Prosperity flows to me all the time.*
> *All the money I spend returns to me multiplied.*

Birthstones

Birthstones are the most commonly worn gemstones today. Stones that relate to people's zodiac signs or the months they were born in are believed to help them overcome weaknesses in their makeup and enhance their positive attributes. The practice of wearing birthstones goes back only a few hundred years, but the original source of the idea dates back to the writings of Josephus in the first century C.E. In *Antiquities of the Jews*, Josephus wrote: "And for the twelve stones [set in Aaron's Breastplate], whether we understand by them the months, or the twelve signs of what the Greeks call the zodiac, we shall not be mistaken in their meaning."[1]

The ancient Greeks assigned different stones for each sign of the zodiac, based on the alleged powers of the stone, its color, and its relationship to the sign. Here is Josephus' list:

- Aries: Bloodstone
- Taurus: Sapphire
- Gemini: Agate
- Cancer: Emerald
- Leo: Onyx
- Virgo: Carnelian
- Libra: Chrysolite
- Scorpio: Beryl
- Sagittarius: Topaz

- Capricorn: Ruby
- Aquarius: Garnet
- Pisces: Amethyst

This selection worked well for a while, but gradually people began associating stones with the months of the year, rather than the signs. Unfortunately, there has always been a great deal of disagreement about the correct stones that should be worn, and a large number of lists have been compiled during the last two thousand years.

Here is the first modern selection of stones for each month of the year. The National Association of Jewelers compiled it in 1912:

- January: Garnet
- February: Amethyst
- March: Bloodstone, Aquamarine
- April: Diamond
- May: Emerald
- June: Pearl, Moonstone
- July: Ruby
- August: Peridot, Sardonyx
- September: Sapphire
- October: Opal, Tourmaline
- November: Topaz
- December: Turquoise, Lapis-Lazuli

This listing is quite different than the earlier European arrangements. Ruby, for instance, was moved from December to July, as it was felt that a red stone would be more appropriate for a summer month. Turquoise was moved from July to December as it was felt that a cool blue stone would be more appropriate for winter. Although it is possible to go along with these changes, the listing still seems rather strange. Neither pearl nor moonstone could be described as warm, but they are placed in June. In fact, pearl appeared only rarely in older lists, as it was considered to be organic matter rather than a stone. Tourmaline did not appear in any of the earlier lists.

This list did not become the standard one, and different groups continued to produce their own lists. In 1937, the National Association of Goldsmiths of Great Britain produced their birthstone list, and the Jewelry Industry Council accepted it in 1952. Since then, this has been the "standard" list:

- January: Garnet
- February: Amethyst
- March: Aquamarine or Bloodstone
- April: Diamond (also Rock Crystal in U.K. list)
- May: Emerald
- June: Pearl, Moonstone (also Alexandrite in U.S. list)
- July: Ruby
- August: Peridot, Sardonyx

- September: Sapphire (also Lapis-lazuli in U.K. list)
- October: Opal (also Pink Tourmaline in U.S. list)
- November: Topaz (also Citrine in U.S. list)
- December: Turquoise (also Zircon in U.S. list)

Unfortunately, although this has become the generally accepted list, it is hard to relate it to the original stones in Aaron's Breastplate. Consequently, you should use the stone that relates to your month of birth only if you happen to like the color, or if it relates to your personal colors derived from your Life Path, Expression, or Soul Urge (see chapter 3).

The stones for each sign of the zodiac are just as hard to determine. Rather than selecting a stone based on a chart that may or may not have any validity, it is better to choose a stone that relates to the color of your zodiac sign. Naturally, you should choose a stone that you find appealing, also. Here are the colors for each sign, with some possible gemstones:

- Aries: Red (Ruby, Red Jasper)
- Taurus: Green (Emerald, Malachite)
- Gemini: Variegated or striped stone (Agate, Banded Onyx, Striped Chalcedony)
- Cancer: Sea-Green (Green Beryl, Green Turquoise)
- Leo: Yellow (Topaz, Zircon)
- Virgo: Apple-Green (Green Feldspar, Green Chrysoprase)

- Libra: Green (Jade, Peridot)
- Scorpio: Red (Bloodstone, Red Carnelian)
- Sagittarius: Blue (Sapphire)
- Capricorn: Dark-Bue, Black (Tourmaline, Black Opal)
- Aquarius: Sky-Blue (Aquamarine, Lapis-Lazuli)
- Pisces: Purple (Amethyst, Purple Fluorspar)

Most of the time you will achieve more magic with a stone that you select for your sign on the basis of color than you will from the gemstones that are listed for your sign in jewelry stores. Even today, these lists don't always agree with each other. While writing this chapter I visited two stores near me to see what their recommendations were. This is what I found:

Sign	Store 1	Store 2
Aries	Bloodstone	Diamond
Taurus	Carnelian	Emerald
Gemini	Pearl	Pearl
Cancer	Chalcedony	Ruby
Leo	Jasper	Sardonyx
Virgo	Emerald	Sapphire
Libra	Beryl	Opal
Scorpio	Amethyst	Topaz
Sagittarius	Topaz	Turquoise
Capricorn	Chrysoprase	Garnet
Aquarius	Rock Crystal	Amethyst
Pisces	Sapphire	Bloodstone

Seasonal Gemstones

To complicate the subject still further, there are also gemstones that have been associated with each of the four seasons. They are:

- Spring: Emerald
- Summer: Ruby
- Autumn: Sapphire
- Winter: Diamond

Gemstones for the Days of Week

Each day of the week is associated with a planet, and this determines the color of the day. Gemstones that relate to these colors can be worn or carried on their particular day to enhance your personal power and energy.

Day	Planetary Ruler	Color
Sunday	Sun	Gold and Yellow
Monday	Moon	White
Tuesday	Mars	Red
Wednesday	Mercury	Blue
Thursday	Jupiter	Purple
Friday	Venus	Green
Saturday	Saturn	Black and White

It is also possible to associate colors with each hour of the day, but for most purposes that is going far too far.

Lithomancy

Lithomancy is the art of divining the future using crystals and gemstones. It is believed to be one of the oldest divination methods, and is mentioned a number of times in the Bible.[2] Many priests and prophets carried an Urim and a Thummim in a pocket on their breastplates. Urim and Thummim were sacred articles, such as gems, crystals, and knucklebones, which were used to answer questions.

There are many methods of practicing lithomancy. One ancient technique was to have a single gem selected. This was placed where light could play on it, and the seer would receive telepathic messages, or see visions in the gemstone. For all intents and purposes, the gemstone was being used as a crystal ball.

My favorite method of lithomancy requires a collection of gemstones. You will need a minimum of forty-five stones, five each of nine colors. I have ten of each color, but started with five. I feel that ten of each color makes a better display and gives the person receiving a reading a much greater choice. Fortunately, tumble-polished stones are not expensive, and you can build up a collection for not much more than the price of a good tarot deck.

You will need stones of the following colors:

- Red: (Red Garnet, Red Jasper, Rhodonite)
- Orange: (Carnelian, Orange Calcite)
- Yellow: (Citrine, Yellow Beryl)
- Green: (Aventurine, Malachite)

- Blue: (Howlite, Lapis Lazuli, Turquoise)
- Indigo: (Iolite, Sodalite)
- Violet: (Amethyst, Purple Garnet)
- Rose/Pink: (Rhodonite, Rose Quartz)
- Gold: (Goldstone, Gold Tiger-Eye)

I have included some suggested stones, as well. As you can see, these are all colors that we discussed in chapter 1. If you wish, you can add other colors, but I feel that nine is a good number. (Numerologically, nine is the number of completion.)

The stones are displayed on a tray, which has been covered with a good quality white or black cloth. I like to have the red stones on the left-hand side of the tray from my client's view. Next to this is a row of orange stones, followed by the others in rainbow order. They make a beautiful display.

The reading can go in several directions. If the client has a question that needs to be answered, he or she may pick a single stone. This is interpreted, based on its color, using the information in chapter one. If necessary, another stone or two can be chosen to add more detail to the answer.

If you are giving brief readings, perhaps to a group of people, you might use three stones. The sitter is asked to choose one stone. This represents his or her past. Another stone is then selected to represent the present. Finally, a third stone is chosen to indicate the future. Once these have been chosen, a reading is given based on the colors that were selected.

Here is an example. Suppose the person selected orange, violet, and red stones. You might say: "In the past you held yourself back a bit. You might have been overly cautious and missed out on opportunities as a result. Right now you are in a violet phase. This means that you are searching for hidden truths and learning more about philosophy and spirituality. It is a learning stage, and it holds great promise for the future, though you may feel unable to move forward at the moment. You are learning useful information for the future. The future is indicated by (red stone). This is a sign of independence and attainment, so you are assured of ultimate success, though it will take a great deal of hard work to get there. However, it will be well worth the effort. Keep learning (indicate the violet stone), use your natural intuition (indicate orange stone), set worthwhile goals (red stone), and make them happen."

These methods involve choosing specific gemstones. An alternate method, which is extremely useful, especially when giving yourself a reading, is to place all the gemstones in a cloth bag. Mix the stones thoroughly in the bag, and then reach in and blindly select a stone. You will be amazed at how accurate this method is. You invariably "choose" the stone or stones that you need to answer your question. I sometimes use this method with other people but prefer to lay the stones out on a tray, as they make such an attractive display.

This is fine for a quick reading, but you will also be asked to give more involved readings. For this, I use the twelve houses of astrology. This is because they cover virtually every area of life:

- 1st House: Self-image, ego
- 2nd House: Personal resources, money, possessions
- 3rd House: Communications, short journeys
- 4th House: Home, parents, domestic matters
- 5th House: Love, children, creativity
- 6th House: Career, health
- 7th House: Spouse, partnerships
- 8th House: Other people's resources, sex, death
- 9th House: Philosophy, education, travel
- 10th House: Public image, parents
- 11th House: Friends, associations, ideals, aspirations
- 12th House: Secrets, enemies, karma

You can ask the querant to select twelve gemstones, one at a time. This can sometimes be a time-consuming process. People often select the first few stones confidently, but then deliberate carefully with the later ones. These are placed in a line in front of him or her. Alternatively, you might like to draw a horoscope wheel, which is a circle divided into twelve sections. The 1st House is the section of the circle that lies between 8 PM and 9 PM, as seen from the querant's perspective. The other houses go in order counterclockwise. This means that the 2nd House lies between 7 PM and 8 PM.

Once the stones have been selected, you can interpret them, providing an in-depth reading which covers twelve areas of the person's life.

Another method of using the horoscope wheel is for the sitter to hold one each of the nine gemstones in his or her hand a few inches above the chart, think of an important question, and then let the gemstones fall. Some will land outside the wheel. These can be discarded, as only gemstones that land inside the circle are interpreted. When you do this, you'll find that some segments of the wheel will contain one, two, or more stones, while other segments have none at all. The stones are interpreted in the same way, relating their color to the interests of the particular house they have landed in.

Your readings will improve with practice. One reason for this is that individual stones will take on interpretations that are meaningful for you. You will no longer be dependent on the color or shape of the stones, or the layout you are using. Each stone will have an assortment of associations for you, in the same way that each tarot card does. Once you reach this stage, your intuition will take over and you will be surprised at the quality of your readings.

Your Color Tree

Gem trees are frequently used in the East as a feng shui remedy. They are believed to increase the luck and prosperity of the occupants of the house, especially if placed in the northwest or southeast parts of the home.

Traditionally, a gem tree is an artificial plant with dozens of semiprecious colored stones attached to it. They make an attractive and colorful display. You can sometimes find gem trees in import stores, but you can easily make your own. An artificial tree can be made from a branch of a dead shrub or a wire bent to create the trunk and branches. Alternatively, you can loosely attach gemstones to a living potted plant. The quantity of gemstones is not as important as the range of colors. Make sure that all the colors of the rainbow are included, and include any other colors that appeal to you.

Place your tree somewhere where you will see it frequently. It will act as a silent affirmation, reminding you each time you see it that it is attracting good luck and prosperity.

While writing this chapter I saw someone using a gem tree to give readings. I was at a large awards function, and a young Asian man was offering readings as part of the entertainment. He asked people who wanted a reading to touch two of the gemstones on the tree. I assume his readings were based on the colors of the gems that were selected. Unfortunately, I was involved in presenting some of the awards and was not able to have a reading, as the line of people waiting their turn was always too long.

In this chapter we have made use of the four elements that have always been used in the West. In the next chapter we will look at the five elements of the East and see how they can be used to enhance your home environment.

CHAPTER THIRTEEN

COLOR IN YOUR HOME

The very word "home" has magical connotations. It is a place of our very own, somewhere where we should feel comfortable, safe, and secure. Here we should be free to be ourselves, and to express ourselves in any way we choose. Color plays an important role in how happy and secure we feel at home as it has a major effect on our physical and emotional health. Ideally, it should uplift and inspire. Color also enables us to create the environment and ambience we want.

It is surprising that many people who are normally confident in their good taste panic when it comes to choosing colors for their home environment. The best approach is to use your instincts and personal preferences, because there are no set rules. You want to feel comfortable and happy in your own home, and any colors that provide this are a good choice for you.

If you live alone, you can use whatever color scheme you wish. However, there are bound to be differences of opinion when more than one person lives in the home. One solution is to use neutral colors in the communal areas and allow the family members to use whatever colors they wish in their own rooms. This sometimes works, but is more likely to create an environment that pleases no one. A better approach is to discuss the color choice first to find points of agreement, and then build on that.

Sometimes, the basic choices will be determined by what is already in the room. You may want to work the color scheme around a favorite rug or built-in furniture. You may choose light colors to lift up a dark and gloomy area.

Your favorite colors may not necessarily be the colors you would choose to have in your home. The colors you ultimately choose will be determined by what you think would work best in the available space, and how you intend to use the room. Your color choices for a calm, restful place will be completely different from those you'd choose for a more exciting, dynamic environment.

You can also use color to create a variety of effects. A dark, gloomy room can be transformed into a warm and inviting place with the right choice of colors. Warm colors can be used to make a large room seem more intimate and inviting. Cool colors make a small, narrow room feel larger.

Spend time thinking about the uses you intend to make of each room. Green, for example, might be a good choice for a room that you will use for study or meditation. However, red would be better for a room that will be used for stimulating activity. Red also works well anywhere that warmth is required. Orange works well in a dining room, as this color aids digestion. Blue has a calming and relaxing effect on people. Deep blue is more relaxing than light blue. Purple is inspirational.

Experiment with swatches of color to choose the shades and tints that will work best for you. Adding white to a color lightens it. This is known as a tint. Likewise, adding black darkens colors. This is called a shade. You are said to be changing a color's tone when you add white or black to it.

Here is a selection of colors that will give you a general idea of what they can do. Of course, the range of tints and shades within each color is enormous.

Red

Red is a stimulating, opulent color that creates movement, activity, and excitement. As it stimulates the appetite and conversation, it can be a good choice for dining rooms. It also works well in hallways and playrooms. It is rich, grand, and powerful, creating an impression of wealth. Red always demands attention. It should not be used in children's bedrooms, as it can make it hard to fall asleep.

Orange

Orange is warm, cheerful, exciting, and full of the joys of life. It is a good choice for any rooms that enjoy plenty of activity, such as hallways, kitchens, dining rooms, living rooms, and family rooms. Orange should not be used in studies and bedrooms.

Yellow

Yellow is warm, bright, cheerful, and invigorating. It can lift up a cold room or any area that receives little or no sun. However, it can appear overpowering when used in a room that already receives a great deal of sunlight. It is a good choice for kitchens, living rooms, and family rooms.

Green

Green is a tranquil, calm, soothing, and harmonious color that is frequently used to connect other colors. (This is because, like violet, it is created from both a warm and a cool color. Green is comprised of yellow, which is warm, and blue, which is cool. Violet comes from warm red and cool blue.) Green works well in kitchens, bedrooms, and warm rooms. It should not be used in rooms that are cold or dark.

Blue

Blue is cool, calm, fresh, soothing, relaxing, tranquil, reflective, and refreshing. It creates a sense of well-being and works well in warm, sunny rooms. Because blue makes people feel relaxed, it is a good choice for bedrooms, kitchens, and bathrooms. It also works well in small rooms, as it makes them seem larger. It should not be used in dining rooms, hallways, or cold rooms.

Violet

Violet is magical, mysterious, and romantic. However, it should be used carefully, as some people find it heavy and draining. You should avoid it if you are feeling insecure. Lilac and lavender make good choices for bedrooms. Violet is usually used as an accent, or as part of a pattern. When used this way it makes the room appear more luxurious.

White

White is pure, innocent, and clean. It is totally neutral, which means that it harmonizes with any other color. It can be used to make a room look larger, and makes a good counterpoint to a strong color. It emphasizes natural light. However, it can sometimes feel cold, especially in rooms that lack natural light. White walls naturally place the focus on paintings and the furniture.

Black

Black absorbs light, and this creates a negative, draining effect. Consequently, it should be used cautiously. It can be useful as an accent to other colors, but because it does not transmit the light we need, it fails to nourish us the way the other colors do.

Pink

Pink is soothing, gentle, caring, romantic, and feminine. Mixing red and white together makes pink. Red is strongly masculine, and it is interesting that the addition of white creates such a totally different energy. Pink works well in bedrooms and any other rooms that are used mainly by the female members of the household.

Natural Colors

Brown is a grounding color. It creates feelings of support and strength. Natural wood is the ideal way to introduce brown into your color scheme. Pottery, ceramics, stones, bricks, and bare plaster are other ways to bring natural colors into the home. They all provide support and stability.

The Five Elements of Feng Shui

Feng shui means "wind and water." It is the ancient Chinese art of living in harmony with your environment. Thousands of years ago, the Chinese found that by building their homes in the right locations (ideally facing south, with gently flowing water in front, and hills behind), they would lead lives of happiness and abundance.[1]

The basic idea behind feng shui is the concept of ch'i, the universal life force, that is in everything. We want the ch'i to flow smoothly throughout the home, creating a positive and stimulating environment. One way we can do this is to use colors that relate to our own personal elements, determined by our year of birth.

The Chinese use a system of five elements: Wood, Fire, Earth, Metal, and Water. You can find your personal element in the appendix. The elements can be looked at in a number of ways. In the Productive Cycle, each element

produces the next. Wood burns and that creates Fire. From
Fire we get ashes, which become Earth. From the Earth we
obtain Metal. Metal can liquefy, and this creates Water.

There is also a Destructive Cycle. Wood drains from the
Earth. Earth absorbs Water. Water puts out Fire. Fire melts
Metal. Metal chops Wood.

Finally, there is a Reduction Cycle. This calms down
the element that follows it in the cycle. It is the Productive
Cycle in reverse: Wood, Water, Metal, Earth, and Fire.

Each element has a large number of associations, including direction and a color or colors:

Element	Direction	Color
Wood	East, Southeast	Green
Fire	South	Red, Purple, and Pink
Earth	Southwest, Northeast, Center	Yellow, Brown, and Orange
Metal	West, Northwest	Silver, White, and Gold
Water	North	Blue, Black, and Gray

You can use the three cycles to help create color harmony
in your home. The best colors for you are those that are
the same as your personal element, or that produce your
element on the Productive Cycle. This also increases the
quantity and quality of personal ch'i in your environment.
If your personal element is Metal, for instance, good colors
for you would include white, silver, and gold, as they relate
to Metal. You would also benefit from having some yellow,

brown, and orange in your environment as they relate to the Earth element, and Earth creates Metal.

You should avoid the colors that relate to the element that destroys your personal element in the Destructive Cycle. For example, if your personal element is Fire, you should avoid blue or black as they relate to the Water element. As you know, Water puts out Fire.

The Reduction Cycle can be used when you want to soften or reduce the effect of a certain element. If your bedroom is in the northeast part of your house, which relates to the Earth element, you might want to add a bit of white to the décor, or perhaps have a white bedspread. This is because Metal calms down Earth in the Reduction Cycle, and this helps ensure a good night's sleep.

You can also use your personal element to determine what clothes would enhance your personal ch'i.

Obviously, different members of the household will have differing personal elements, and this can be addressed in the rooms that the family members use most. Personal bedrooms, for instance, should reflect the occupant's personal element, as well as the element that precedes it in the Productive Cycle. Children's bedrooms should contain the color of the element that precedes theirs in the Productive Cycle. This is because they are still growing, and the element that precedes theirs helps them mature and develop.

You can enhance the effect of the elements in each direction of your home by adding furniture, ornaments, or wall coverings of the correct colors in that area. You can energize a room by adding the color that produces the element color of the room. A Fire room, for instance, is red. You can stimulate the red energy by adding anything that is green (as Wood produces Fire in the Productive Cycle). However, decorating a house using the colors for each direction should be done with caution. A house can feel uncomfortable when every room is decorated in a different color. It is better to have a general color scheme, and add accents to enhance the ch'i energy by adding colors that relate to the directions.

Chinese Astrology Colors

Each of the twelve animals in the Chinese horoscope has a number of associations, including a color. You can use this color in your home environment, in addition to your personal color. However, if the colors clash in the Destructive Cycle, you should use your personal element from your year of birth in preference to the color that relates to your horoscope animal.

Animal	Element	Color
Rat	Water	Black
Ox	Earth	Yellow
Tiger	Wood	Green
Rabbit	Wood	Green
Dragon	Earth	Yellow
Snake	Fire	Red
Horse	Fire	Red
Sheep	Earth	Yellow
Monkey	Metal	White

Rooster	Metal	White
Dog	Earth	Yellow
Boar	Water	Black

The Japanese system of astrology is called *Kigaku*, which means "science of the spirit." It uses the same animal symbols as Chinese astrology, but provides additional colors using a combination of your element and animal sign. Here are all the possible combinations in this system:

- Water Rat: White
- Wood Rat: Green
- Fire Rat: Red
- Wood Ox: Turquoise and Sky Blue
- Metal Ox: White
- Fire Ox: Purple
- Earth Tiger: Yellow, Black, and White
- Water Rabbit: White
- Wood Rabbit: Green
- Metal Rabbit: Red
- Wood Dragon: Turquoise and Sky Blue
- Metal Dragon: White
- Fire Dragon: Purple
- Earth Snake: Black, Yellow, and White
- Water Horse: White
- Wood Horse: Green

- Metal Horse: Red
- Wood Sheep: Turquoise and Sky Blue
- Metal Sheep: White
- Fire Sheep: Purple
- Earth Monkey: Black, Yellow, and White
- Water Rooster: White
- Wood Rooster: Green
- Metal Rooster: Red
- Wood Dog: Turquoise and Sky Blue
- Metal Dog: White
- Fire Dog: Purple
- Earth Boar: Black, Yellow, and White

These colors can be used in any rooms that you use frequently. They also work well when worn on occasions in which you need to feel successful and in control.

CHAPTER FOURTEEN

YOUR COLOR DIARY

It can be a valuable and revealing exercise to keep a color diary. You can keep a special diary for this purpose if you wish. I use the diary I keep by the phone. I also keep a container of colored pencils beside the phone. Every evening, usually before going to bed, I'll think about the day I've just had, and give it a color. I don't spend any time thinking about what color to use. It is spontaneous. I grab the crayon that seems appropriate for the day, and draw a small square of this color on the correct diary page. Sometimes, it will occur to me during the day that this day happens to be orange, or blue, or whatever. Most of the time, I give it no thought at all, and I'm sometimes surprised with my color choice.

Your color of the day will be revealing right away, but will become more valuable as time goes by. After keeping your diary for a while, you'll be able to look back over a month or two and see what colors were important in your life during that period. Your diary allows you to keep track of the ups and downs in your life, as these will be revealed by your color choices.

You may find that one or two colors predominate. Conversely, you may find that you've used all the colors you have in your collection of pens. It is more likely that your color choices will be largely warm (red, orange, yellow) or cool (green, blue, violet). You may find that you are subconsciously selecting complementary colors (red/green, orange, blue, or yellow/purple). These colors will be balancing themselves out in your life.

You should also check to see if any colors are missing. Every color of the rainbow has a positive effect on you, and any missing colors mean you are not gaining the energy you need from them.

Missing Colors

Red

It is a sign of exhaustion when red is missing. You may be ill or overtired. You need to improve your diet, ensure that you get enough sleep, and take some exercise to gradually raise your energy levels to where they should be.

Orange

Your confidence and self-esteem are likely to be low if orange is missing. Eat orange fruits and vegetables, breathe in orange energy, and undertake movement that involves your lower abdomen. Dancing would be perfect, but any movement helps to stimulate the area of your sacral chakra.

Yellow

If yellow is missing, you are likely to be nervous or suffering from stress. Breathe in yellow energy, and massage the area just above your navel.

Green

An absence of green usually indicates relationship problems. Take a leisurely walk in a park, and enjoy the healing that comes from all the greens you will see. If possible, walk barefooted on the grass.

Blue

If blue is missing, it is likely that you feel unsupported or let down by someone close to you. Breathe in blue energy, and go for a walk anywhere where there is water. Sitting beside a fountain is just as beneficial as walking along a beach.

Indigo

An absence of indigo is a sign that you are being taken advantage of, or are not fully appreciated, by people close to you. Take some time out by yourself, and breathe in indigo energy.

Purple

If purple is missing you have temporarily lost contact with your spiritual self. Spend some time alone in a place that seems spiritual to you. Listen to uplifting music and inhale purple energy.

Color Bathing

A highly effective way to recoup a missing color is to enjoy a leisurely bath in colored water. You can use food coloring for this, or colored bath salts, if you can find them in the colors you need.

Make the most of your colored bath. Allow plenty of time. You may want to play gentle music, burn candles, and perhaps add a few drops of essential oils to the water. The water should be hot enough for comfort, but not too hot. Use good quality towels to make the bath time as luxurious as possible.

Visualize the color you are bathing in, and picture it entering every cell of your body, filling you with energy and vitality. Relax in the bath for as long as you wish. When you feel ready, get out, and dry yourself briskly with the towel. Stretch luxuriously, get dressed, and relax for a few minutes before carrying on with your day.

You will find color baths invigorating, healing, and balancing. Enjoy them frequently. You do not need to wait until your diary tells you it is time for a color bath. You can enjoy one any time you feel the need for a certain color.

CHAPTER FIFTEEN

CONCLUSION

I hope that after reading this book you will look at colors with different eyes. You will be like Joseph with his cloak of many colors, and experience the beneficial effects of color everywhere you go.

As you now know, you can use color in many different ways to enhance your life. Experiment with different colors. Try wearing a color that you wouldn't normally choose for a day or two, and observe the effects it has on you. Use color to understand yourself better, to gain access to your inner self, and to divine the future. Experiment with color when meditating or working magic. Make good use of color for mental, emotional, spiritual, and physical health.

Conclusion

Julian Grenfell (1888–1915), an English soldier and poet who died of wounds in World War I, understood color well when he wrote: "Life is Colour and Warmth and Light."[1] For him, life itself was composed of three elements, all of which relate to color. Without color, life would be incredibly drab, and there would be little warmth or light.

Fortunately, we live in a world that is teeming with color. A rainbow of color is waiting to enhance every aspect of your life. Make good use of it.

APPENDIX

Elements and Signs for the Years 1900 to 2000

Element	Sign
Metal	Rat: 31 January 1900 to 18 February 1901
Metal	Ox: 19 February 1901 to 7 February 1902
Water	Tiger: 8 February 1902 to 28 January 1903
Water	Rabbit: 29 January 1903 to 15 February 1904
Wood	Dragon: 16 February 1904 to 3 February 1905
Wood	Snake: 4 February 1905 to 24 January 1906
Fire	Horse: 25 January 1906 to 12 February 1907
Fire	Sheep: 13 February 1907 to 1 February 1908
Earth	Monkey: 2 February 1908 to 21 January 1909

Earth	Rooster: 22 January 1909 to 9 February 1910
Metal	Dog: 10 February 1910 to 29 January 1911
Metal	Boar: 30 January 1911 to 17 February 1912
Water	Rat: 18 February 1912 to 5 February 1913
Water	Ox: 6 February 1913 to 25 January 1914
Wood	Tiger: 26 January 1914 to 13 February 1915
Wood	Rabbit: 14 February 1915 to 2 February 1916
Fire	Dragon: 3 February 1916 to 22 January 1917
Fire	Snake: 23 January 1917 to 10 February 1918
Earth	Horse: 11 February 1918 to 31 January 1919
Earth	Sheep: 1 February 1919 to 19 February 1920
Metal	Monkey: 20 February 1920 to 7 February 1921
Metal	Rooster: 8 February 1921 to 27 January 1922
Water	Dog: 28 January 1922 to 15 February 1923
Water	Boar: 16 February 1923 to 4 February 1924
Wood	Rat: 5 February 1924 to 24 January 1925
Wood	Ox: 25 January 1925 to 12 February 1926
Fire	Tiger: 13 February 1926 to 1 February 1927
Fire	Rabbit: 2 February 1927 to 22 January 1928
Earth	Dragon: 23 January 1928 to 9 February 1929
Earth	Snake: 10 February 1929 to 29 January 1930
Metal	Horse: 30 January 1930 to 16 February 1931
Metal	Sheep: 17 February 1931 to 5 February 1932
Water	Monkey: 6 February 1932 to 25 January 1933
Water	Rooster: 26 January 1933 to 13 February 1934
Wood	Dog: 14 February 1934 to 3 February 1935
Wood	Boar: 4 February 1935 to 23 January 1936
Fire	Rat: 24 January 1936 to 10 February 1937

Fire	Ox: 11 February 1937 to 30 January 1938
Earth	Tiger: 31 January 1938 to 18 February 1939
Earth	Rabbit: 19 February 1939 to 7 February 1940
Metal	Dragon: 8 February 1940 to 26 January 1941
Metal	Snake: 27 January 1941 to 14 February 1942
Water	Horse: 15 February 1942 to 4 February 1943
Water	Sheep: 5 February 1943 to 24 January 1944
Wood	Monkey: 25 January 1944 to 12 February 1945
Wood	Rooster: 13 February 1945 to 1 February 1946
Fire	Dog: 2 February 1946 to 21 January 1947
Fire	Boar: 22 January 1947 to 9 February 1948
Earth	Rat: 10 February 1948 to 28 January 1949
Earth	Ox: 29 January 1949 to 16 February 1950
Metal	Tiger: 17 February 1950 to 5 February 1951
Metal	Rabbit: 6 February 1951 to 26 January 1952
Water	Dragon: 27 January 1952 to 13 February 1953
Water	Snake: 14 February 1953 to 2 February 1954
Wood	Horse: 3 February 1954 to 23 January 1955
Wood	Sheep: 24 January 1955 to 11 February 1956
Fire	Monkey: 12 February 1956 to 30 January 1957
Fire	Rooster: 31 January 1957 to 17 February 1958
Earth	Dog: 18 February 1958 to 7 February 1959
Earth	Boar: 8 February 1959 to 27 January 1960
Metal	Rat: 28 January 1960 to 14 February 1961
Metal	Ox: 15 February 1961 to 4 February 1962
Water	Tiger: 5 February 1962 to 24 January 1963
Water	Rabbit: 25 January 1963 to 12 February 1964
Wood	Dragon: 13 February 1964 to 1 February 1965

Wood	Snake: 2 February 1965 to 20 January 1966
Fire	Horse: 21 January 1966 to 8 February 1967
Fire	Sheep: 9 February 1967 to 29 January 1968
Earth	Monkey: 30 January 1968 to 16 February 1969
Earth	Rooster: 17 February 1969 to 5 February 1970
Metal	Dog: 6 February 1970 to 26 January 1971
Metal	Boar: 27 January 1971 to 15 January 1972
Water	Rat: 16 January 1972 to 2 February 1973
Water	Ox: 3 February 1973 to 22 January 1974
Wood	Tiger: 23 January 1974 to 10 February 1975
Wood	Rabbit: 11 February 1975 to 30 January 1976
Fire	Dragon: 31 January 1976 to 17 February 1977
Fire	Snake: 18 February 1977 to 6 February 1978
Earth	Horse: 7 February 1978 to 27 January 1979
Earth	Sheep: 28 January 1979 to 15 February 1980
Metal	Monkey: 16 February 1980 to 4 February 1981
Metal	Rooster: 5 February 1981 to 24 January 1982
Water	Dog: 25 January 1982 to 12 February 1983
Water	Boar: 13 February 1983 to 1 February 1984
Wood	Rat: 2 February 1984 to 19 February 1985
Wood	Ox: 20 February 1985 to 8 February 1986
Fire	Tiger: 9 February 1986 to 28 January 1987
Fire	Rabbit: 29 January 1987 to 16 February 1988
Earth	Dragon: 17 February 1988 to 5 February 1989
Earth	Snake: 6 February 1989 to 26 January 1990
Metal	Horse: 27 January 1990 to 14 February 1991
Metal	Sheep: 15 February 1991 to 3 February 1992
Water	Monkey: 4 February 1992 to 22 January 1993

Water	Rooster: 23 January 1993 to 9 February 1994
Wood	Dog: 10 February 1994 to 30 January 1995
Wood	Boar: 31 January 1995 to 18 February 1996
Fire	Rat: 19 February 1996 to 6 February 1997
Fire	Ox: 7 February 1997 to 27 January 1998
Earth	Tiger: 28 January 1998 to 15 February 1999
Earth	Rabbit: 16 February 1999 to 4 February 2000
Metal	Dragon: 5 February 2000 to 23 January 2001
Metal	Snake: 24 January 2001 to 11 February 2002
Water	Horse: 12 February 2002 to 31 January 2003
Water	Sheep: 1 February 2003 to 21 January 2004
Wood	Monkey: 22 January 2004 to 8 February 2005
Wood	Rooster: 9 February 2005 to 28 January 2006
Fire	Dog: 29 January 2006 to 17 February 2007
Fire	Boar: 18 February 2007 to 6 February 2008
Earth	Rat: 7 February 2008 to 25 January 2009
Earth	Ox: 26 January 2009 to 13 February 2010

NOTES

Introduction

1. Alice Cunningham Fletcher, "Indian Ceremonies." Cambridge: Peabody Museum, 1883. (Article in *The XVI Report of the Peabody Museum of American Archaeology and Ethnology*.)
2. Augustine Hope and Margaret Walch, *The Color Compendium* (New York: Van Nostrand Reinhold, 1990), 242.
3. E. Schachtel, *Metamorphosis* (New York: Basic Books, Inc., 1959), 109.
4. Victoria Finlay, *Colour: Travels through the Paintbox* (London: Hodder and Stoughton Limited, 2002), 217.

5. Wassily Kandinsky, *Concerning the Spiritual in Art* (New York: Dover Publications, Inc., 1977), 25. (Originally published in 1914 as *The Art of Spiritual Harmony*.)

6. Olivier Messiaen, quoted in *The Color Compendium* by Augustine Hope and Margaret Walch (New York: Van Nostrand Reinhold, 1990), 284.

7. Tricia Guild, *Tricia Guild on Colour* (London: Conran Octopus Limited, 1992), 15.

Chapter One

1. Reenu Boyatzis, "Children's Emotional Associations with Colors." Article in *Journal of Genetic Psychology*, Vol. 155, March 1994, 77.

2. Augustine Hope and Margaret Walch, *The Color Compendium*, xiii.

3. Paul Zealanski and Mary Pat Fisher, *Colour for Designers and Artists* (London, The Herbert Press Limited, 1989), 33.

4. Editors of Time-Life Books, *Mysteries of the Unknown: Magical Arts* (Alexandria, VA: Time-Life Books, 1990), 129.

5. Alec Gill, *Superstitions: Folk Magic in Hull's Fishing Community* (Beverley, UK: Hutton Press Limited, 1993), 99.

6. Faber Birren, *Color in Your World* (New York: Collier Books, revised edition 1978), 110.

7. Suzy Chiazzari, *The Complete Book of Colour* (Shaftesbury, UK: Element Books Limited, 1998), 25.

8. Belinda Recio, *The Essence of Red* (Salt Lake City: Gibbs-Smith, Publisher, 1996), 13–16.

9. Philippa Waring, *A Dictionary of Omens and Superstitions* (London, UK: Souvenir Press, 1978), 64.

Chapter Five

1. Reuben Amber, *Color Therapy* (Santa Fe: Aurora Press, 1983), 54–55.

2. Dinshah P. Ghadiali, *Spectro-Chrome Metry Encyclopedia* (3 volumes)(Malaga, NJ: Spectro-Chrome Institute, 1933).

3. International Association of Colour, 46 Cottenham Road, Histon, Cambridge CB4 9ES, United Kingdom. Their website is: www.internationalassociationofcolour. com.

4. R. Gerard, "Differential Effects of Colored Lights on Psychophysiological Functions." Article in *American Psychology*, 13, 340.

5. Brian Ward, *ESP: The Sixth Sense* (London: Macdonald Educational Limited, 1980), 59.

6. Swami Panchadasi, *The Human Aura* (Chicago: Yoga Publication Society, 1915), 46–47.

Chapter Eight

1. Jennifer Warner, *Meditation May Bolster Brain Activity.* http://content.health.msn.com/content/ article/96/103943.htm

Chapter Nine

1. C. G. Jung, *Memories, Dreams, Reflections* (New York: Pantheon Books, 1963), 196.

Chapter Ten

1 Josephus, quoted in Faber Birren, *Color Psychology and Color Therapy* (Secaucus, NJ: The Citadel Press, 1961), 6.
2. Richard Webster, *Amulets and Talismans for Beginners* (St. Paul: Llewellyn Publications, 2004).

Chapter Eleven

1. Florence Farr, quoted in Mary Greer, *Women of the Golden Dawn: Rebels and Priestesses* (Rochester: Park Street Press, 1995), 64.
2. Plato (translated by H. D. P. Lee), *Timaeus* (Harmondsworth, UK: Penguin Books Limited, 1965), 67.

Chapter Twelve

1. Josephus, quoted in Rupert Gleadow, *The Origin of the Zodiac* (New York: Atheneum, 1969), 131.
2. Exodus 28:30, Numbers 27:21, and 1 Samuel 28:6.

Chapter Thirteen

1. More information on feng shui can be found in *Feng Shui for Beginners* by Richard Webster (St. Paul: Llewellyn Publications, 1997) and *101 Feng Shui Tips for the Home* by Richard Webster (St. Paul: Llewellyn Publications, 1998).

Chapter Fifteen

1. Julian Grenfell, *Into Battle* (first published in *The Times* London, May 28, 1915). This poem can be found in many anthologies of poets from the Great War.

SUGGESTED READING

Abbott, Arthur G. *The Color of Life.* New York: McGraw Hill Book Company, Inc., 1947.

Andrews, Ted. *How to See and Read the Aura.* St. Paul: Llewellyn Publications, 1991.

———. *How to Heal With Color.* St. Paul: Llewellyn Publications, 1992.

Argüelles, José and Miriam. *Mandala.* Boston: Shambhala Publications, Inc., 1985.

Babbitt, Edwin S. *The Principles of Light and Color: The Healing Power of Color.* New Hyde Park: University Books, Inc., 1967.

Bailey, Alice A. *Esoteric Psychology, Volume 1.* New York: Lucis Publishing Company, 1936.

Birren, Faber. *Color in Your World.* New York: Macmillan Publishing Co., Inc., 1962.

―――. *Color Psychology and Color Therapy.* Secaucus: The Citadel Press, 1961.

―――. *New Horizons in Color.* New York: Reinhold Publishing Corporation, 1955.

―――. *The Symbolism of Color.* Secaucus: Citadel Press, 1988.

Bomford, David, and Roy Ashok. *Colour.* London: National Gellery, 2000.

Brooker, Don. *Electromagnetic Colour Healing: The Challenge.* Cambridge, N.Z.: A. D. Brooker, 2000.

Buckland, Raymond. *Color Magick: Unleash Your Inner Powers.* St. Paul: Llewellyn Publications, 1983.

Cameron, Julia. *The Artist's Way: A Spiritual Path to Higher Creativity.* Los Angeles: Jeremy P. Tarcher, Inc., 1992.

Chevreul, M. D. *The Principles of Harmony and Contrast of Colours.* London: Bell & Daldy, Limited, 1870.

Copony, Heita. Translated by Gabrielle Bertelmann. *Mystery of Mandalas.* Wheaton: Quest Books, 1989. (First published as *Das Mysterium Des Mandalas* by Aquamarin Verlag.)

Cunningham, Scott. *Cunningham's Encyclopedia of Crystal, Gem and Metal Magic.* St. Paul: Llewellyn Publications, 1988.

Dahlke, Rudiger. *Mandalas of the World.* New York: Sterling Publishing Company, 1992.

Don, Frank. *Color Your World.* New York: Destiny Books, 1977.

Ferrucci, Piero. *What We May Be: Techniques for Psychological and Spiritual Growth Through*

Psychosynthesis. Los Angeles: Jeremy P. Tarcher, Inc., 1982.

Finlay, Victoria. *Colour: Travels Through the Paintbox*. London: Hodder and Stoughton Limited, 2002.

Ganim, Barbara, and Susan Fox. *Visual Journaling: Going Deeper than Words*. Wheaton: Quest Books, 1999.

Goethe, Johann Wolgang von. *Theory of Colors*. Cambridge: The M.I.T. Press, 1970.

Guild, Tricia. *Tricia Guild on Colour*. London: Conran Octopus Limited, 1992.

Heline, Corinne. *Color and Music in the New Age*. La Canada: New Age Press, Inc., 1964.

Houston, Jean. *The Search for the Beloved: Journeys in Mythology and Sacred Psychology*. New York: Jeremy P. Tarcher/Putnam, 1987.

Hunt, Roland. *The Eighth Key to Colour*. London: L. N. Fowler Limited, 1965.

Judith, Anodea. *Wheels of Life: A User's Guide to the Chakra System*. St. Paul, Llewellyn Publications, 1987.

Jung, C. G. *Mandala Symbolism*. Princeton: Princeton University Press, 1972.

———. *Memories, Dreams, Reflections*. Recorded and edited by Aniela Jaffé. Translated by Richard and Clara Winston. London: Collins and Routledge & Kegan Paul, 1963.

Kargere, Audrey. *Color and Personality*. York Beach: Samuel Weiser, Inc., 1982.

Keyte, Geoffrey. *The Mystical Crystal: Expanding Your Crystal Consciousness*. Saffron Walden, UK: The C. W. Daniel Company Limited, 1993.

Kunz, George Frederick. *The Curious Lore of Precious Stones*. New York: J. B. Lippincott Company, 1913.

Ladd-Franklin, Christine. *Colour and Colour Theories.* New York: Harcourt, Brace and Company, Inc., 1929.

Lansdowne, Zachary F. *The Rays and Esoteric Psychology.* York Beach: Samuel Weiser, Inc., 1989.

Loynes, Jesse. *Colour Dynamics.* London: Jesse Loyndes, 1976.

Lüscher, Max. *The Lüscher Color Test.* New York: Pocket Books, Inc., 1971.

Mann, John, and Lar Short. *The Body of Light.* Rutland: Charles E. Tuttle Company, Inc., 1990.

Newton, Isaac. *Opticks: or, a Treatise of the Reflexions, Refractions, Inflexions and Colours of Light.* London: Sam. Smith and Benj. Walford, 1704.

Ouseley, S. G. J. *The Power of the Rays.* London: L. N. Fowler and Company Limited, 1951.

Perkins, James S. *Visual Meditations on the Universe.* Wheaton: Quest Books, 1984.

Recio, Belinda. *The Essence of Blue.* Salt Lake City: Gibbs-Smith, Publisher, 1996.

———. *The Essence of Red.* Salt Lake City: Gibbs-Smith, Publisher, 1996.

Sargent, Walter. *The Enjoyment and Use of Color.* New York: Charles Scribner's Sons, Inc., 1923.

Slate, Joe H. *Aura Energy for Health, Healing and Balance.* St. Paul: Llewellyn Publications, 1999.

Stuber, William C. *Gems of the 7 Color Rays.* St. Paul: Llewellyn Publications, 2001.

Walker, Dr. Morton. *The Power of Color.* New York: Avery Publishing Group, 1991.

Webster, Richard. *101 Feng Shui Tips for the Home*. St. Paul: Llewellyn Publications, 1998.

————. *Aura Reading for Beginners*. St. Paul: Llewellyn Publications, 1998.

————. *Candle Magic for Beginners*. St. Paul: Llewellyn Publications, 2004.

————. *Feng Shui for Beginners*. St. Paul: Llewellyn Publications, 1997.

————. *Pendulum Magic for Beginners*. St. Paul: Llewellyn Publications, 2002.

————. *You Are a Rainbow*. Auckland, NZ: Brookfield Press, 1991.

Wills, Pauline. *Colour Healing Manual*. London: Judy Piatkus (Publishers) Limited, 2000.

Wright, Angela. *The Beginner's Guide to Colour Psychology*. London: Kyle Cathie Limited, 1995.

Wright, W. D. *The Measurement of Colour*. London: Adam Hilger Limited, 1944.

INDEX